THE
Female Advocate

The Juvenilia Press Editions

The Juvenilia Press promotes the study of literary juvenilia, a category of literature that has been largely neglected. Its editions are slim volumes of early writings by children and adolescents (up to the approximate age of 20), including published and unpublished works of children: both those who achieved greatness as adults and those who did not become adult writers but whose writing is full of percipience and zest.

Founded in 1994 by Juliet McMaster at the University of Alberta in Edmonton, the Press has been based in the Faculty of Arts and Social Sciences at the University of New South Wales in Sydney since 2001, and has an international team of contributing editors from Britain, Canada, Japan, New Zealand, the United States, and Australia.

Each volume is devoted to a specific author and edited by an expert in the field, with the assistance of one or more students, usually postgraduates. Student involvement in the research and editorial process is an essential part of the pedagogic aim of the Juvenilia Press; and the illustrations, often executed by young aspiring artists or by the original young authors themselves, aim to capture the tone of the original productions. By contributing to the recovery, publication, and critical exploration of childhood writings, the Juvenilia Press actively promotes literary research and the professional development of students. At the same time, we endeavour to provide, for a wide audience, an insight into the creative energy of this rich and varied body of writing.

Christine Alexander
General Editor and Director

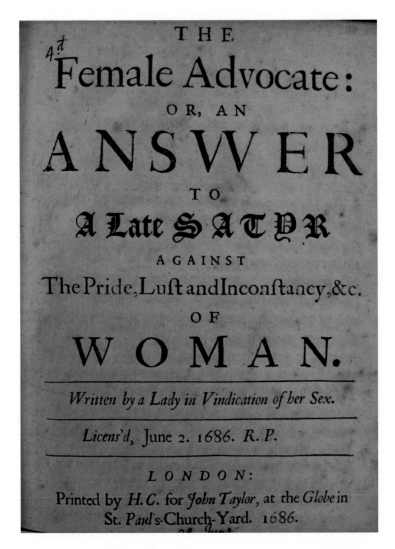

THE
4ᵗ Female Advocate:
OR, AN
ANSWER
TO
𝔄 𝔩𝔞𝔱𝔢 𝔖𝔄𝔗𝔜ℜ
AGAINST
The Pride, Luſt and Inconſtancy, &c.
OF
WOMAN.

Written by a Lady in Vindication of her Sex.

Licens'd, June 2. 1686. R. P.

LONDON:
Printed by *H. C.* for *John Taylor,* at the *Globe* in
St. *Paul's*-Church-Yard. 1686.

Title page of the first edition of The Female Advocate, *from the copy held at the Chawton House Library, Chawton, Hampshire, UK.*

THE
Female Advocate:

or, an Answer to a Late Satyr
Against The Pride, Lust and Inconstancy, &c.
of Woman.

Written by a Lady in Vindication of her Sex.

[BY "S.F.", SARAH FYGE EGERTON]

edited by Peter Merchant, with Steven Orman

Juvenilia
PRESS

Sydney, Australia

Sarah Fyge Egerton's The Female Advocate
ISBN: 978 0 7334 2808 1

Contents of the present edition, including text, editorial matter
and notes, copyright © 2010 Christine Alexander, General Editor,
Juvenilia Press, School of English Media and Performing Arts, FASS,
University of New South Wales, Sydney, NSW 2052, Australia.

Cover image: "The Faithful Wives of Weinsberg", late sixteenth-
century engraving by Zacharias Dolendo after Jacques de Gheyn II.
Cover and interior design: Winston Pei, Black Riders Design

CONTENTS

ACKNOWLEDGEMENTS

Steven Orman's contribution to this volume was vital. He lent invaluable assistance with the illustrations and also improved the annotation, although the responsibility for any errors or shortcomings that may remain in the Notes is mine alone.

For any felicities I owe a very considerable debt of gratitude to Professor Christine Alexander and Professor Juliet McMaster, whose suggestions about what I had drafted were invaluable.

The thanks of everybody involved in preparing the edition go out to Canterbury Christ Church University, for a very timely grant from its Research Office towards the production costs.

The Juvenilia Press would like to thank the Chawton House Library for help in obtaining a photograph of the title page to *The Female Advocate*.

Peter Merchant

ILLUSTRATIONS

Frontispiece: Title page of the first edition of *The Female Advocate*, from the copy held at the Chawton House Library, Chawton, Hampshire, UK.

1. "Eva" (1666-7), a wooden bust by Alonso Cano. Courtesy of Granada Cathedral.

2. "Lais Corinthiaca" (1526), a painting by Hans Holbein the Younger, by permission of the Kunstmuseum in Basel, Switzerland. Photo by Martin P. Bühler, Kunstmuseum Basel.

3. "The Suicide of Lucretia" (1666), a painting by Rembrandt. Courtesy of the Minneapolis Institute of Arts: The William Hood Dunwoody Fund.

4. "The Faithful Wives of Weinsberg", a late sixteenth-century engraving by Zacharias Dolendo after Jacques de Gheyn II.

5. Illustration from a printed broadside ballad, "A Statute for Swearers and Drunkards", dating from 1624, contained in the Samuel Pepys Collection. Courtesy of the Pepys Library at Magdalene College, Cambridge.

6. "Recipe for Marital Bliss" (c. 1680), a German woodcut attributed to Abraham Bach of Augsburg; reproduced from Dorothy Alexander and Walter L. Strauss, *The German Single-Leaf Woodcut, 1600–1700*. Courtesy of Abaris Books.

INTRODUCTION

Surveying more than fifty poetic careers for his *Lives of the Poets* (1779–81), Samuel Johnson found that three particular prodigies stood out: "Cowley, Milton, and Pope, are distinguished among the English Poets by the early exertion of their powers" (2: 238). The "learned puerilities" of these famous fast developers appear "scarcely credible" in boys so young, he ventured (1: 2-3), or are "not easily conceived to have been attainable" (2: 236). Necessarily omitted from Johnson's exclusively male field, however, was a poet who as a teenager in 1686 had shown herself no less remarkable a young achiever than Milton and Cowley before her and almost as precocious a lisper in numbers as Pope later became. That poet was Sarah Fyge (afterwards Sarah Egerton); and it was into a work entitled *The Female Advocate* (*FA* for the purposes of all parenthetical documentation in what follows) that she had poured her poetic precocity.

Unfortunately, Egerton's own claim that she was only fourteen when she wrote *The Female Advocate* (see lines 288-90 of the text, and endnote 89) cannot be independently verified. A year or two would be the very most that she could have subtracted from the real figure, however, if attempting to make her achievement seem even more impressive than it already was. Sixteen is the upper limit which the best biographical guesses about the author set upon her age at the time of the poem's first publication, in 1686. For although there is no documentary evidence showing exactly when Egerton was born—and an additional complication is that throughout her lifetime official records were numbering the years according to the old (pre-1752) style of calendar, whereby 25 March was New Year's Day—her probable date of birth is in the early months of, as we would reckon it, 1670.

She was born Sarah Fyge, apparently one of six daughters in the family of a London physician. The respectability which came with that household and upbringing, evaporated, however, on the appearance of *The Female Advocate*. Far from feeling any paternal pride in his daughter's poem, Thomas Fyge seems to have viewed it as an act of open defiance. It stood up for women, as its title indicates; and it tilted with unmaidenly tenacity and vehemence at an existing poem, the anonymously published *Love given o're* (London, 1682/3), which had disparaged them. Fyge's daughter had rushed in where she should have feared to tread, therefore, with an impetuous challenge to the writer of an obscene satire; and she had offered her response quite openly, descending into the marketplace in order to do so. That she was identified as the author of *The Female Advocate* only by her initials, not by her full name, could not suffice to expunge the shame and the disgrace. That she subsequently would not own to having ever consented to—let alone chosen or pressed for—the publication of the first edition (see "To the Reader" and endnote 4) was apparently not accepted as any excuse for so brazen a breaking of cover and so serious a breach of filial faith. Rustication, Fyge resolved, was the punishment which best fitted his daughter's offence. Having been sent to live with relatives in the country, she married (perhaps before she was even out of her teens) an attorney called Edward Field—only to resume her poetic career, no longer as "S.F." but as "Mrs. S. F.", when her husband died. By 1703, she was married again—but unhappily—to her second cousin Thomas Egerton, a country rector with seven children already to his name. The last twenty years of her life were spent in Buckinghamshire, first as the rector's wife and then (from 1720) as his widow; and they appear to have passed with little further exertion of her once precocious poetic powers. She died in 1723.

Elizabeth Kowalewski-Wallace's *Their Fathers' Daughters*, tracing in eighteenth-century women writers "the dual feminine motivations of anger against and desire for what patriarchy offers women" (9), offers one possible way of approaching and understanding the story of Egerton's life. The various lockings of horns to which that life led her, both inside the home and in print, may serve to show that she never ceased to need—yet always needed to resist—some powerful male antagonist. He might be her husband, or before that her father, or he might be the satirical renouncer of love and denouncer of women whom Egerton in her preface to *The Female Advocate* could identify not by name but simply as "my Antagonist." In fact the anonymous author whose *Love given o're* had so raised the young Egerton's hackles was Robert Gould (c.1660–c.1709).[1] Gould's poem is patently calculated to provoke: a searingly sardonic farewell to the "whining Curse" of love (*LGO* 1), and a warning to all men to shun the company of women. The speaker has banished "faithless *Silvia*" forever from his breast (*LGO* 1). Though "lov'd, and fair", she has "prov'd false and perjur'd, and unkind" (*LGO* 9). With her are banished "all the thoughts of Womankind" (*LGO* 1), or at least all thoughts of marrying; and every male reader should, for his own good, make the same sacrifice. He should be taught by "all their various sorts of Vice" (*LGO* 2), which Silvia epitomises, to avoid women "as [he] wou'd the pains of Hell" (*LGO* 12):

> For not the wild destructive waste of War,
> Nor all the endless Lab'rinths of the Bar,
> Famine, Revenge, perpetual loss of health,
> No nor that grinning Fiend Despair it self,
> When it insults with most tyranick sway,
> Can plague or torture Mankind more than they. (*LGO* 11)

All of this railing against women runs true to type as the invective of the conventional betrayed lover or the equally conventional figure of the lover who, like Shakespeare's Posthumus, is hellishly furious because he mistakenly supposes himself scorned. In *Cymbeline*, Posthumus launches his tirade with "Is there no way for men to be, but women/ Must be half-workers?" and goes on to complain that "even to vice/ They are not constant, but are changing still" (Shakespeare, *Cymbeline*, 2.5.1-2 and 29-30). Gould's poem turns the same blazing anger upon the same traditional targets. "How happy had we been", it muses, "had Heav'n design'd/ Some other way to propagate our kind" (*LGO* 2). And again:

> They now inconstant in their Follies prove,
> Ev'n as inconstant as they do in Love:
> Nor is't alone confin'd in those to range,
> Their Vices too themselves admit of change... (*LGO* 11).

We cannot know whether Egerton read *Love given o're* as a direct outpouring of personal bile or purely as a dramatic exercise, a work doing as (for instance) Tennyson's "Locksley Hall" would later do: invent an embittered lover and have him speak out of a particular situation quite separate, and maybe quite remote, from the poet's own. Nor can we know whether the indignation in Egerton's response is counterfeited and conventional—a conscious climbing into the kit prescribed in this rhetorical game for players on both sides—or genuine and heartfelt. In any case, her dissent from the injurious imaginings of another writer lays a basis more solid than she might otherwise have had for significant imaginative creation of her own. Implicitly, that is, within Egerton's energetic rebuttal in *The Female Advocate* of the false images of women which a previous poem had painted—as, for example, within Jane Austen's challenge in *Northanger Abbey* to the false images of women's lives being put about by Gothic romance—are contained the authentic accents of a new, but already authoritative, artistic voice.

By 1686, most of the necessary conditions for the emergence of this new voice were securely in place. Not only was the argument set up by *Love given o're* one which Egerton's growing confidence and broadening experience, as she put childhood behind her, now entitled her to join, but the course of seventeenth-century history itself appeared peculiarly conducive to the sort of statement she would make with *The Female Advocate*. As an expanding awareness of the world came with the age that Egerton had reached, so a taste for disputation came from the age in which she lived, with James II on the throne and a new Declaration of Indulgence imminent (1687, amended 1688). It seemed now that liberty of conscience and freedom of speech were to be asserted and exercised as the common entitlements of every citizen, even on matters which could never have admitted them before. The same ferment of ideas that consequently surrounded denominational difference, and produced a poem like John Dryden's *The Hind and the Panther* (1687), surrounded gender politics too. Although the most celebrated contemporary attempt at the redressing of the wrongs of woman—Mary Astell's *Some Reflections upon Marriage*—did not appear until 1700, there was already a growing inclination to expose and challenge misogynistic prejudice, and an empowering sense that the forces of resistance had begun to gather. *Love given o're* having very forcefully put one position on women, it was incumbent on *The Female Advocate* to ensure that the opposite view was aired with a polemical power which matched Gould's own. Egerton's poem was to be a form of "the 'countercheck quarrelsome'", as Shakespeare's Touchstone defines it, giving Gould the lie and meeting his satirical strike with a controlled but ferocious retaliation. In 1686, not only the year of *The Female Advocate* but the year that saw Isaac Newton's *Principia* licensed for publication, what seemed to hold sway was Newton's third law of motion: for every action, an equal and opposite reaction.

Egerton's poem is thus a perfect example of what an essay by Margot Norris (whose details are duly noted in my list of "Works Cited and Consulted") has termed the "female back answer". Having initially appointed herself the Female Advocate, Egerton assumes the prosecuting counsel's role by levelling as much against men as *Love given o're* alleged against women. She takes the game to the opposition by turning the same fire on her male "Antagonist" that his own poem turned on what it called "the lewd Sex" (*LGO* 1). The symmetry of that exchange, if not its finer detail, is captured in a single-leaf woodcut of this period (c.1680) by Abraham Bach of Augsburg. Bach's woodcut (reproduced below, as Illustration number 6) divides like a diptych into a left-hand and a right-hand side—respectively, a husband chastising his wife and a wife chastising her husband—which mirror each other exactly. *The Female Advocate* applies the principles of proportionate requital and chiastic reversal no less systematically, since Egerton's poem is a point-by-point and measure-for-measure response to Gould's. With "Woman, ye Powers! The very name's a Charm" (*FA*, line 68) it converts into "charm" what Gould's poem had condemned as "crime": "Woman! by Heav'ns the very Name's a Crime" (*LGO* 2). It comprehensively undoes his catalogue of all the "various sorts of Vice" (*LGO* 2) to which women are supposedly prone. Female "Pride, Lust, and Inconstancy" had of course been Gould's chief themes, with the catalogue commencing *in medias res*: "Womans unbounded Lust I'le first proclaim" (*LGO* 3). Particularly to be proclaimed was "our late illustrious *Bewley*", who "enroll'd more Females in the List of Whore, / Than all the Arts of Man e're did before"; and now there are other embodiments of lust besides, for "*Cresswold*, and *Stratford*, the same path do tread" (*LGO* 4, 5). (The three women named here—Betty Buly, Madam Cresswell, and Sarah Stratford—were all noted bawds.) Next in the catalogue is pride, a vice which women are charged with having enthroned in their hearts as "the Deity they most adore" (*LGO* 6). However, because women are changeable even in respect of their "dearest darling Vices", lust and pride, their primary defining characteristic—and the thing "for which they most are Fam'd"—is inconstancy (*LGO* 11, 8).

Egerton counters each one of these charges. Her "true Verse" turns the tables on her antagonist's "spiteful Rhime" (*FA*, line 295) by strenuously contending that female so-called vice is caused only by the misapprehensions—or the coercion—of men. Generally women's vices are outweighed by the vices of men, just as the virtues of women outshine the corresponding qualities in a man:

> In Constancy they men excell as far
> A[s] heavens bright lamp doth a dull twinckling star ....
> > She's all divine
> And by a splendid lustre doth outshine
> All masculine souls ....
> Thus what I've said doth plainly shew there are
> Men more impious than a woman far ....
> > Man more false than Woman is,
> More unconstant, nay and more perfidious ....
> (*FA*, lines 137-8, 430-32, 465-6, 638-9)

Some women—such as the exceptional and egregious "*Bewly, Stratford*, nay and *Chreswell* too" (*FA*, line 246)—may indeed embody the worst that humanity can sink to; but in no way does this support Gould's spiteful satire on theirs as "the lewd Sex" (*LGO* 1). Rather, what Egerton takes it to show is that women embody the best in humanity too; for the worst, according to a proverb familiar at the time, is the corruption of the best. Egerton must of course also reject her opponent's reading of Eve and the Eden myth: woman as "the Original of Mischief," as the preface to *Love given o're* provocatively puts it, and "Th' original, and spring of all [man's] Strife" (*LGO* 10). Eve, for Egerton, is actually less at fault than Adam: "*Adam* did most of the Guilt partake .... Man's knowing most, doth his Sin make most large" (*FA*, lines 43, 49). If a woman and a man fall equally short of moral perfection, more blame attaches to the man because of the advantages with which he began.

Egerton's position on Eve was not in fact a new one. The view that Eve might be less culpable than Adam had been voiced by (among others) Æmilia Lanyer, whose 1611 poem *Salve Deus Rex Judaeorum* puts in a plea on Eve's behalf:

> But surely *Adam* can not be excusde,
> Her fault though great, yet hee was most too blame....
> (lines 777-8).

When Egerton took up this position three-quarters of a century later, however, there was an altogether sharper drawing of the battle lines: on the figure of Eve, very obviously, because of John Milton's epic treatment in *Paradise Lost* (first published in 1667); and equally, because the cultural climate of the 1680s was so favourable to all kinds of disputation, on the broader issues of the social roles—and moral and intellectual capacities—of women in general. Concentrated into the lash and backlash of Gould's "Satyr" and Egerton's rejoinder, therefore, is the essence of that long series of exchanges between the detractors and defenders of women, played out across Europe and over the entire early modern period, which has come to be characterised as the *querelle des femmes*. Egerton was among those responsible for the sudden steep escalation in this that scholars examining the latter part of the period have sensed: "at the end of the seventeenth century women joined the *querelle des femmes* and even began an equivalent or *querelle des hommes*" (Capern 2).

The composition of *The Female Advocate* in this way coincides with a perceptible picking up of the pace at which, first, long litanies of complaints would come from antifeminist campaigners—and then, following that, counterblasts to their poems or pamphlets would be engineered by (or on behalf of) the women they had maligned. The intensity of these exchanges could be felt in 1678, for instance, when Samuel Butler concluded his poem *Hudibras* with a power struggle between the disputatious hero and a widow whose fortune he covets. He writes to her stating that "women first were made for men,/ Not men for them" ("An Heroical Epistle of Hudibras to His Lady", lines 273-4); and she, in "The Lady's Answer to the Knight" (lines 239-40), comes back with "Though women first were made for men,/ Yet men were made for them again". What is released in the verse satires of Butler and his contemporaries is all of the stored power which over the space of hundreds of years had gone into the articulation of the "female back answer". Three centuries before Egerton came to read *Love given o're*, Geoffrey Chaucer was already articulating it, and in a choice of styles: earnest and protracted in *The Legend of Good Women* ("Why noldest thow as wel han seyd goodnesse/ Of wemen, as thow hast seyd wikednesse?"), dramatic and physical in *The Wife of Bath's Prologue* ("I with my fest so took hym on the cheke/ That in oure fyr he fil backward adoun").[2]

The polemic tradition in which Gould and Egerton appear proud to stand not only begins long before their own ventures into print but extends for at least a century beyond. The respective arguments of *Love given o're* and *The Female Advocate* about women's inconstancy or (conversely) women's encapsulation of "all that's pious, chast and true,/ Heroick, constant, nay, and modest too" (*FA*, lines 368-9) were to be resumed by a close contemporary of Egerton's, Richard Steele (1672–1729), in a *Spectator* paper dated 13 March 1711 (*Selections* 463-7). The piece is a narrative diptych whose second part is a reversed image of what went before. First, Steele's female advocate (given the name of Arietta) is subjected to a diatribe from a visitor to her home who "in his Talkative Way" dilates upon "the old Topick, of Constancy in Love". He seeks to show that all women are perfect strangers to this by trotting out "the celebrated Story of the *Ephesian* Matron", unfaithful to the memory of her dead husband almost as soon as her mourning begins. It is one of the stories used in *Love given o're*, where Gould brings a gleeful relish to his account of the "lewd Act" with which the Matron "made a Brothel of her Husband's Tomb" (*LGO* 9-10). Steele comes up with a cogent "Counterpart to the *Ephesian* Matron", however, by having Arietta tell the story of Inkle and Yarico, in which an Englishman basely betrays an Indian maid's total trust in him. The previous (and prejudiced) depiction of inconstant women is answered from a partisan female perspective, and the pendulum swings decisively back towards the perfidy of men.

The dialogues that Egerton enters into with *Love given o're*, or Arietta with her visitor, continue—transferred to territory more comic than those combatants occupied—in the fiction of Jane Austen. Chapter 23 of Austen's *Persuasion* (1818) has Captain Harville trying to argue that women are more prone to inconstancy than men are, but Anne Elliot refusing to concede the point because she realises his evidence is tainted; wherever books appear to bear him out, "the pen has been in [men's] hands". Anne's reversion to a grievance of Arietta's—"You Men are Writers, and can represent us Women as Unbecoming as you please in your Works, while we are unable to return the Injury" (*Selections* 464)—may indicate that, for the duration of the *querelle*, an opportunity to wield the pen and so "return the Injury" is what some women most desire. By the time Arietta voiced her frustrations, that process of returning the injury had in fact already started, as the evidence of booksellers' lists alone might serve to show; *The Female Advocate* itself had by then been joined by the first of no fewer than four eighteenth-century works (by "Eugenia", "a Lady of Quality", 1700; William Woty, 1770; Mary Scott, 1774; and Mary Anne Radcliffe, 1799) which share Egerton's title. By the time Austen was out of her teens, a major landmark in the process had been reached, in the shape of a work—Mary Wollstonecraft's *Vindication of the Rights of Woman*—which attempted two operations simultaneously: a championing of women, and an avenging.

Although Wollstonecraft's *Vindication* is of course in prose where Egerton's had been in verse, there is as much to connect as to separate the two works. The publishers of both were based in St Paul's Churchyard. The first edition of each was brought out with such hectic haste, it would appear, as obliged the author to produce a more considered and correct second edition soon afterwards. Wollstonecraft's rueful reflections on this, "had I allowed myself more time I could have written a better book, in every sense of the word" (quoted in Tomalin 136), parallel

Egerton's admission in her preface to the second edition of *The Female Advocate* that if the first "had been intended for the Press, some things there inserted, had been left out; which I have now done".[3] Egerton differs from Wollstonecraft, however, in having never inserted her full name. The title page of *A Vindication of the Rights of Woman* would carry Mary Wollstonecraft's; but on the title page of *The Female Advocate* the "Lady" writing "in Vindication of her Sex" is anonymous, and Egerton's name (Sarah Fyge, as it then was) is reduced at the end of the prefatory address "To the Reader" to its initial letters. This reticence is not at all surprising in a girl only half the age that Wollstonecraft would be at the time of her *Vindication*, necessarily without any previous literary career or reputation, and in fear of her father. Such reticence, moreover, had distinct advantages; and probably far more is gained than is lost by the suppression of a name which, in any case, none of the poem's purchasers could have recognised. The individual is merged in the collective, to allow the poem (especially where its discourse is centred on "we" and "our") to speak not with one voice but with many. Nor is the "by a Lady" label any kind of automatic limitation. Margaret Ezell has shown that, while such labels are commonly affixed to their work by women writers in this period, they are often far from promising anything conventionally ladylike in the attitudes which the work expresses. Indeed, texts describing themselves as written "by a Lady" are "frequently less conciliatory than contrary in their relationship to the status quo" (Ezell 77).

Here is the foundation of what would seem a fair finding about the strategy followed by "S.F.": that convention informs but does not inhibit her writing in *The Female Advocate*. Whether or not any of Egerton's indignation is feigned, the poem in the end does far more to distance itself from convention than *Love given o're* had cared to do. Gould's poem makes a positive virtue of its reliance upon routine railing, standard debating points and well-worn instances like the celebrated story of the Ephesian matron. In order that it can crush completely women's pretensions to anything better than folly or vice, it insists on mobilising as much as it can of the tradition in which it stands; and the whole weight of that tradition is brought down upon the foe with mechanical remorselessness. Egerton on the other hand appears committed to resisting—so far as she is able—all recourse to the prefabricated, and refraining from the mechanical rehearsal of commonplaces. Whatever looked like lazy thinking would risk undermining the poem's project. *The Female Advocate* needs to be packed with overt logical structures; section has to be linked to section by the favourite fastening words ("For", "So", "Then", "Thus") of forensic demonstration; and Egerton must concentrate on advancing original arguments, however knotty these may turn out to be, rather than repeating familiar ones. By making a poem which all the world will know was written "by a Lady" as thoughtful and firmly organised a piece as possible, she will refute the dismissive stereotype that describes women as capricious and unamenable to reason. Aside from its immediate responses to the charges of female "Pride, Lust, and Inconstancy", part of the purpose of *The Female Advocate* is demonstrating women's readiness—and hunger—for much more than they are currently confined to in the field of intellectual endeavour. In this way it can make the sort of demands, and display the kind of determination, which Egerton's later poem "The Emulation" (Lonsdale 31-2) sees her consolidating: "We will our rights in learning's world maintain".

This is not to say that *The Female Advocate*, however strenuous the thinking which went into it, and whatever gestures it might make towards logical consistency and rigour, pretends to be elaborately crafted verse. Another of Egerton's later poems (quoted here in endnote 89) stated that the first version of *The Female Advocate* had been dashed off "in less time than fourteen days"; and, at such speed as that, some rough edges would be inevitable. The likelihood of Egerton "inserting" some careless or incautious passages was further increased by the fact of her writing at that point (as the same statement again affirms) "Without Design of Publication", and thus for her manuscript to be privately circulated rather than scrutinised by a large general readership. Although she was certainly capable—despite her youth—of a more polished performance, such polishing might have been to the detriment both of the poem's impact in Egerton's lifetime and of its revelatory value now. It is precisely where there is some rhythmic stutter in the verse, or the creak of a badly carpentered couplet, that the surge of partisan sentiment is most strongly sensed and the energy with which Egerton is championing "her Sex" becomes most vividly apparent. In certain of its lines (as is argued in endnote 147), *The Female Advocate* makes incoherence eloquent; and the impression left by the moments of incoherent anger in it is that the text must be driven by absolutely authentic feelings and grievances.

Rude and rough-hewn as it therefore is, *The Female Advocate* bows only to such evaluative criteria as arise from its own specific character and occasion; the rules to which it submits are not quite the normal rules of verse-making, nor those of standard speech-making, but rather those of something which at once is both of the above and neither. According to W. B. Yeats (1865–1939), "We make out of the quarrel with others, rhetoric, but of the quarrel with ourselves, poetry".[4] And what one very determined first-time author proved it possible to make out of the *querelle des femmes* in 1686 was a perfect platform from which to launch a lively challenge to the "spiteful Rhime" of *Love given o're* and on which to begin building the sort of literary career that either her seniors then or her poetic successors might envy. "I think it is good Frugality for young Beginners to send forth a small Venture at first", Egerton's prefatory address "To the Reader" concedes, as they take arms against a "merciless Ocean of Criticks"; but, even as she dampens expectation and prepares us to hear no more from her than the faint splash of some speculative skiff, this particular young beginner shows she means business by putting to sea in a pocket battleship.

Notes

1. The author (a friend of John Oldham's) is discussed, and the work reproduced in facsimile, in Laura L. Runge (ed.), *Texts from the Querelle, 1641–1701* (1), as detailed in the list of Works Cited and Consulted. All quotations are taken from the text printed here. The full title of the work is *Love given o're: or, a Satyr against the Pride, Lust, and Inconstancy, & c. of Woman* (London, 1682/3)—hereafter abbreviated, for the purposes of parenthetical referencing, to *LGO*.

2. *The Legend of Good Women*, Prol. G, 268-9; *The Wife of Bath's Prologue*, 792-3. My quotations are taken from F. N. Robinson (ed.), *The Works of Geoffrey Chaucer*, 490, 83.

3. The second edition of *The Female Advocate* is reproduced in facsimile in *Texts from the Querelle, 1641–1701* (1), directly after *Love given o're*. My quotation (in which the second "had been" has the force of "would have been") is taken from the second of two unnumbered pages making up the prefixed notice "To the Reader".

4. See W. B. Yeats, *The Major Works*, ed. Edward Larrissy, 411.

NOTE ON THE TEXT

Copies of the 1686 first edition of *The Female Advocate* are extremely scarce, but among the UK libraries holding it are the British Library, London (where its shelfmark is 840.h.40), and Chawton House Library, Chawton, Hampshire (Writers' Sequence EGE). These are the copies against which the text that follows has been checked. It reproduces what was printed in 1686, except that the obvious typographical oddities of the original—such as spacing errors, or the lower-case letters with which for no apparent reason four lines of verse (lines 105, 111, 165, and 181) begin—have been corrected and some particularly distracting misprints removed. The letter W (which in the seventeenth century was often printed in the divided form, as a double V) has been modernised. Lower-case "s" has been converted from the obsolete long form of the letter, which is commonly (though not constantly) used in the 1686 edition, to the standard short form. The triplet braces used originally to mark places in the text where three lines (rather than two lines) are bound by rhyme have been deleted. In all other respects the wording and appearance of the first published edition have been retained, including those inconsistencies in spelling, in capitalisation, in elision, and in the use of possessive apostrophes which are commonly found in this period. (Between the two lines that have "yeilds"—lines 150 and 427—comes, for instance, one—line 179—that has "yields"; "Heaven" in line 7 is followed by "Heav'n" in line 9; in line 138 we find "heavens bright lamp," but in line 261 "heaven's Majesty"; and "won't...compare" in line 361 sits alongside "wont do" in line 501.) The explanatory endnotes which are added to the text address any more unusual and mystifying anomalies or apparent deficiencies.

My Introduction touches upon the puzzles which surround the first edition of *The Female Advocate* and make its status somewhat problematic. Egerton claimed not to have authorised its publication, and it was not until a second edition appeared in 1687 that (while still not controlling it completely) she had a chance to check and correct the text. Then, complaining in her preface that the transcribers and compositors had either not managed or not even tried to decipher her original ("they that had the Charge of it, in the room of blots, writ what they pleas'd, and much different from my Intention"), she made several passages more easily intelligible—and/or smoother metrically—than they had been in the first edition. For that reason, my explanatory endnotes must make occasional reference to the 1687 readings of particular lines. The reasons for nevertheless basing the text printed in the present volume upon the 1686 edition have to do with its being more unguarded and therefore potentially more revealing than the replacement text of 1687. The intemperate touches of the first edition sometimes speak volumes, as Egerton of course recognised when she went back over the "things ... inserted"—despite their being "not fit to be exposed to every eye"—while she was blissfully unaware that the poem would ever go to press and, just to be on the safe side, duly eliminated them.

After 1687, the next edition of *The Female Advocate* appeared in 1706 (the year Egerton's father died), although it bore the date 1707. This edition regularised some of the spelling and punctuation, making more use of the possessive apostrophe; it had a number of words beginning with capital letters which had not done so before, as well as vice versa; and it corrected several of the misprints with which the poem was previously sprinkled (while also introducing a handful of new ones). The effect was to leave students of *The Female Advocate* with three texts to juggle, by creating a second successor to the 1686 original. Neither of the two renders the other (or, still less, the 1686 original) superfluous; so variant readings from both, where they are of any consequence, are duly recorded in the endnotes below, and—according to the point in the poem's textual history at which the revision was first effected—they are indicated by the bracketed date (1687) or (1707).

NOTE ON THE ILLUSTRATIONS

The illustrations for this volume have all been chosen to suggest the entrenched positions of both sides in that phase of the *querelle des femmes* which precedes the publication in the 1680s first of the poem Egerton sets herself to answer, Robert Gould's *Love given o're* (*LGO*), and then of her own *Female Advocate* (*FA*). From those hostile to women came the allegation, as Egerton summarises it, that they "engross all/ That's either fickle, vain or whimsical"; to those seeking to defend women, on the other hand, they stood for whatever is "pious, chast and true,/ Heroick, constant, nay, and modest too". As Bronwen Price observes, this attribution to women of heroic constancy—accompanied by the suggestion that men are degenerate and inconstant—involves "reversing traditional categories of gender difference" (Price 298).

Illustration number 1 is a wooden bust by Alonso Cano (but finished by Juan Vélez de Ulloa), which dates from 1666–7 and may be seen in the cathedral of Granada, Spain. It depicts Eve, the debate over whom sharply divides the two sides of the *querelle*. For John Milton in *Paradise Lost*, published just as Cano was carving this image, the name Eve chimes with "evil" ("O Eve, in evil hour thou didst give ear / To that false worm …"); but "how could *Eve* be bad?" (*FA*, line 37) was Egerton's question twenty years later.

Illustration number 2 is a painting by Hans Holbein the Younger, "Lais Corinthiaca" (1526). Like Eve, Lais of Corinth was routinely vilified in antifeminist contributions to the *querelle*. Egerton's mention of Lais (*FA*, line 508) acknowledges the opposing side's use of her not as a singular exception but as a representative specimen, a byword for the weakness and wickedness of the whole of womankind. This kind of generalising was essential to denunciations like Robert Gould's, of women as "universally … Dispos'd to Mischief" (*FA*, lines 75-6).

The next pair of illustrations, numbers 3 and 4, draw

on classical and medieval history to depict two of the acts commonly cited and celebrated by writers on the feminist side of the *querelle*, when they told the stories of women who were right-minded, resourceful, and resolute.

Illustration number 3 shows, just at the moment when the shame of Tarquin's having violated her leads her to kill herself, "the chast *Lucretia*" (*FA*, line 121)—although to Chaucer in his *Legend of Good Women* (and, subsequently, to Shakespeare) she was "Lucrece". The painting is by Rembrandt and, dating as it does from 1666, precedes by just twenty years the first appearance of Egerton's poem.

Illustration number 4 is a late sixteenth-century Dutch engraving. It shows the faithful wives of Weinsberg, to whose story Egerton devotes ten verse lines (*FA*, lines 152-61) and whom she proudly pits against the far from faithful women pointed to by Robert Gould.

The final pair of illustrations, numbers 5 and 6, are seventeenth-century images of the female avenger, the very role in which Egerton herself would be cast by a title page that made her both advocate and vindicatress: "The Female Advocate: or, an Answer to a Late Satyr Against the Pride, Lust and Inconstancy, &c. of Woman. Written by a Lady in Vindication of her Sex".

Illustration number 5 is part of a printed broadside ballad, "A Statute for Swearers and Drunkards", which dates from 1624. The woodcut depicts a wife standing up to her errant husband and laying on her reproaches with a ladle as she warns him that another night in his cups might mean a spell in the stocks.

Illustration number 6 is drawn—by kind permission of the publisher—from Dorothy Alexander and Walter L. Strauss, *The German Single-Leaf Woodcut, 1600–1700* (New York: Abaris Books, 1977), 61. The original woodcut (attributed to Abraham Bach and dated at around 1680) consists of, on one side, the image of a husband chastising his wife for talkativeness and other failings allegedly typical of women, while on the other side the image is reversed to show a wife chastising her husband for failings (including drunkenness) which are seen as typically male.

THE
Female Advocate:
OR, AN
ANSWER
TO
𝔄 𝔏𝔞𝔱𝔢 𝔖𝔄𝔗𝔜ℜ
AGAINST
The Pride, Lust and Inconstancy, &c.
OF
WOMAN.

Written by a Lady in Vindication of her Sex.

Licens'd, June 2. 1686. *R. P.*

LONDON:
Printed by *H. C.* for *John Taylor,* at the *Globe* in
St. *Paul's*-Church-Yard. 1686.

To the *READER.*

That which makes many Books come abroad into the World
without Prefaces, *is, the only Reason that incites me to one,*
viz. *the Smalness of them; being willing to let my Reader know*
why this is so: For as one great Commendation of our Sex, is, to
know much, and speak little, *so my* Virgin-Modesty *hath*
put a Period to the intended Length of the ensuing Lines,[1] *lest*
censuring Criticks should measure my Tongue by my Pen, and
condemn me for a Talkative,[2] *by the length of my* Poem. *Tho'*
I confess the Illustrious Subject requires (nay commands) an
enlargement from any other Pen than mine (or those under
the same Circumstances) but I think it is good Frugality for
young Beginners to send forth a small Venture at first, and
see how that passes the merciless Ocean of Criticks, and what
Returns it makes, and so accordingly adventure the next time.
I might enlarge this Preface with the common Excuse of Writers
for the Publication of their Books, viz. *the Importunities*
of her obliging Friends:[3] *But what it was put me upon the*
Publication of this,[4] *I am not bound to give the Reader an*
Account of; but I think the Debauchery which I now answer,
is a sufficient warrant for this appearing of mine;[5] *in which*
he doth not only exclaim against Virtue, but Moral Honesty
too,[6] *and would (were it alone sufficient) banish all Goodness*
out of them; but that will be an impossible thing, so long as
we (the most essentially good) do subsist: for 'tis observed in
all Religions, that Women are the truest Devotionists, and

the most pious, and more heavenly than those who pretend to be the most perfect and rational Creatures;[7] for many Men with the Conceit of their own Perfections, neglect that which should make them so; as some mistaken persons, who think if they are of the right Church they shall be infallibly saved,[8] when they never follow the Rules which lead to Salvation; and when Persons with this Inscription pass currant in Heaven,[9] then it will be according to my Antagonist's Fancy, that all Men are good, and fitting for Heaven because they are Men; and Women irreversibly damn'd, because they are Women: But that Heaven should make a Male and Female, both of the same Species, and both indued with the like Rational Souls, for two such differing Ends, is the most notorious Principle, and the most unlikely of any that ever was maintained by any Rational Man, and I shall never take it for an Article of my Faith, being assured that Heaven is for all those whose Purity and Obedience to its Law, qualifies them for it, whether Male or Female; to which Place the latter seem to have the Claim,[10] is the Opinion of one of its Votaries,

S. F.

Blasphemous Wretch, who canst[11] think or say
Some Curst or Banisht Fiend usurp't the way[12]
When *Eve* was form'd; for then's deny'd by you
Gods Omniscience and Omnipresence too:[13]
5   Without which Attributes he could not be,
The greatest and supreamest Deity:
Nor can Heaven sleep, tho' it may mourn to see
Degenerate Man utter Blasphemy.[14]
When from dark *Chaos* Heav'n the World did make,
10 Made all things glorious it did undertake;[15]
Then it in *Eden*'s Garden freely plac'd[16]
All things pleasant[17] to the Sight or Taste,
Fill'd it with Beasts & Birds, Trees hung with Fruit,
That might with Man's Celestial Nature suit:
15 The World being made thus spacious and compleat,
Then Man was form'd, who seemed nobly great.
When Heaven survey'd the Works that it had done,
Saw Male and Female, but found Man alone,
A barren Sex, and insignificant;
20 So Heaven made Woman to supply the want,
And to make perfect what before was scant:
Then surely she a Noble Creature is,
Whom Heaven thus made to consummate all Bliss.[18]
Though Man had Being first, yet methinks She
25 In Nature should have the Supremacy;
For Man was form'd out of dull senceless Earth;
But Woman she had a far nobler Birth:
For when the Dust was purify'd by Heaven,
Made into Man, and Life unto it given,
30 Then the Almighty and All-wise God said,
That Woman of that Species should be made:

Which was no sooner said, but it was done,
'Cause 'twas not fit for Man to be alone.[19]
Thus have I prov'd Womans Creation good,
35 And not inferior, when right understood:
To that of Man's;[20] for both one Maker had,
Which made all good; then how could *Eve* be bad?
But then you'l say, though she at first was pure,
Yet in that State she did not long endure.
40 'Tis true; but if her Fall's examin'd right,
We find most Men have banish'd Truth for spight:[21]
Nor is she quite so guilty as some make;[22]
For *Adam* did most of the Guilt partake:
For he from God's own Mouth had the Command;[23]
45 But Woman she had it at second hand:
The Devil's Strength weak Woman might deceive,
But *Adam* tempted only was by *Eve*.
Eve had the strongest Tempter, and least Charge;[24]
Man's knowing most, doth his Sin make most large.
50 But though Woman Man to Sin did lead[25]
Yet since her Seed hath bruis'd the Serpent's Head:[26]
Why should she be made a publick scorn,
Of whom the great Almighty God was born?
Surely to speak one slighting Word, must be
55 A kind of murmuring Impiety:
But still their greatest haters[27] do prove such
Who formerly have loved them too much:
And from the Proverb they are not exempt;
Too much Familiarity has bred Contempt;
60 For they associate themselves with none,
But such whose Virtues like their own, are gone;
And with all those, and only those who be

1. "Eva" (1666-7), wooden bust by Alonso Cano.

Most boldly vers'd in their Debauchery:[28]
And as in *Adam* all Mankind did die,
65 They make all base for ones Immodesty;[29]
Nay, make the Name[30] a kind of Magick Spell,
As if 'twould censure married Men to Hell.[31]

Woman, ye Powers! the very Name's a Charm,
And will my Verse against all Criticks arm.
70 The *Muses* or *Apollo* doth inspire
Heroick Poets; but your's is a Fire,[32]
Pluto from Hell did send by *Incubus*,
Because we make their Hell less populous;
Or else you ne'er had damn'd the Females thus:
75 But if so universally they are[33]
Dispos'd to Mischief, what need you declare
Peculiar Faults, when all the World might see
With each approaching Morn a Prodigy:[34]
Man curse dead woman; I could hear as well[35]
80 The black infernal Devils curse their Hell:
When there had been no such place[36] we know,
If they themselves had not first made it so.
In Lust perhaps you others have excell'd,
And made all Whores that possibly would yield;
85 And courted all the Females in your way,
Then did design at last to make a Prey
Of some pure Virgins; or what's almost worse,
Make some chaste Wives to merit a Divorce.[37]
But 'cause they hated your insatiate Mind,
90 Therefore you call what's Virtuous, Unkind:
And Disappointments did your Soul perplex;
So in meer spight you curse the Female Sex.

2. Hans Holbein the Younger, Laïs Corinthiaca, 1526 (acc.no. 322)
Lime wood, 34.5 x 27 cm

I would not judge you thus, only I find
You would adulterate all Womankind,[38]
95 Not only with your Pen; you higher soar;
You'd exclude Marriage, make the World a Whore.

But if all Men should of your Humor be
And should rob *Hymen* of his Deity,[39]
They soon would find the Inconveniency.
100 Then hostile Spirits would be forc'd to Peace,
Because the World so slowly would increase.
They would be glad to keep their Men at home,[40]
And each want more to attend his Throne:
Nay, should an *English* Prince resolve that he
105 Would keep the number of's Nobility:[41]
And this dull custom some few years maintain'd,
There would be none less than a Peer oth' land.
And I do fancy 'twould be pretty sport
To see a Kingdom cramb'd into a Court.[42]
110 Sure a strange world, when one should nothing see,
Unless a Baudy House or Nunnery.[43]
Or should this Act ere pass,[44] woman would fly
With unthought swiftness, to each Monastry
And in dark Caves secure her Chastity.
115 She only in a Marriage-Bed delights;
The very Name of *Whore* her Soul affrights.
And when that sacred Ceremony's gone,
Woman I am sure will chuse to live alone.

There's none can number all those vertuous Dames
120 Which chose cold death before their lovers flames.[45]
The chast *Lucretia* whom proud *Tarquin* lov'd,

3. "The Suicide of Lucretia" (1666), painting by Rembrandt. Courtesy of the Minneapolis Institute of Arts, The William Hood Dunwoody Fund.

Her he slew,[46] her chastity she prov'd.
But I've gone further than I need have done,
Since we have got examples nearer home.
125 Witness those *Saxon* Ladies who did fear

The loss of Honour when the *Danes* were here:[47]
And cut their Lips and Noses that they might
Not pleasing seem, or give the *Danes* delight.
Thus having done what they could justly do,
130   At last they fell their sacrifices too.
Thus when curst *Osbright* courted *Beon*'s wife,[48]
She him refus'd with hazard of her life.
And some which I do know but will not name,
Have thus refus'd and hazarded the same.
135   I could say more, but History will tell
Many more things that do these excel.

In Constancy they men excell as far[49]
A heavens bright lamp[50] doth a dull twinckling star.
Tho' man is alwaies altering of his mind,
140   Inconstancy is only in womankind.[51]
'Tis something strange, no hold, it isn't[52] because
The men have had the power of making Laws;
For where is there that man that ever dy'd,
Or ere expired with his loving Bride.[53]
145   But numerous trains of chast wives expire
With their dear Husbands, tho in flames of fire:[54]
We'd do the same if custom did require.
But this is done by *Indian* women,[55] who
Do make their Constancy immortal too,
150   As is their Fame: We find *India* yeilds
More glorious *Phoenix* than the *Arabian* fields.[56]
The *German* women Constancy did shew[57]
When *Wensberg* was besieg'd, beg'd they might go
Out of the City, with no bigger Packs
155   Than each of them could carry on their Backs.

The wond'ring world expected they'd have gone
Laded with treasures from their native home,
But crossing expectation each did take
Her Husband as her burden on her back.
160 So saved him from intended death, and she
At once gave him both life and liberty.
How many loving wives have often dy'd:
Drownded in tears by their cold husbands side.[58]
And when a Sword was Executioner,
165 The very same hath executed her,
With her own hands; eagerly meeting death,
And scorn'd to live when he was void of breath.[59]
If this isn't Constancy, why then the Sun
With Constant Motion don't his progress run.[60]
170 There's thousands of examples that will prove,
Woman is alwayes Constant in chast Love.
But when she's courted only to some Lust,
She well may change, I think the reason's just.[61]
Change did I say, that word I must forbear,
175 No, she bright Star wont wander from her sphere[62]
Of Virtue (in which Female Souls do move)
Nor will she joyn with an insatiate love.[63]
For she whose first espoused to vertue[64] must
Be most inconstant, when she yields to lust.
180 But now the scene is alter'd,[65] and those who
Were esteemed modest by a blush or two,
Are represented quite another way,
Worse than mock-verse doth the most solid Play.[66]
She that takes pious Precepts for her Rule,
185 Is thought by some a kind of ill-bred fool;
They would have all bred up in *Venus* School.[67]

4. "The Faithful Wives of Weinsberg", late sixteenth-century engraving by Zacharias Dolendo after Jacques de Gheyn II.

I. de Geyn inven,
Sach. Dolendo schulp
Visscher excude

De Vrouwen van Winberge
De Keyser heeft de stadt, de Keyser
Wy zyn in s'vyants wil end' in zen
Ons mannen gaen ter doot : en al h
En heeft haer aievers toe dan tot d

Mans op den rugghe wt de Stadt draeghende.

And when that by her speech or carriage, she
Doth seem to have sence of a Deity,
She straight is taxt with ungentility.[68]
190 Unless it be the little blinded Boy,[69]
That Childish god, *Cupid*, that trifling toy,
That certain nothing, whom they feign to be
The Son of *Venus* daughter to the Sea.
But were he true, none serve him as they shoud,
195 For commonly those who adore this god,
Do't only in a melancholy mood;
Or else a sort of hypocrites they are,
Who do invocate him[70] only as a snare.
And by him they do sacred love pretend,
200 When as heaven knows, they have a baser end.
Nor is he god of love; but if I must
Give him a title, then he is god of lust.
And surely Woman impious must be
When e're she doth become his votary,
205 Unless she will believe without controul,
Those that did hold a Woman had no Soul:[71]
And then doth think no obligation lyes
On her to act what may be just or wise.[72]
And only strive to please her Appetite,
210 And to embrace that which doth most delight.
And when she doth this paradox believe,
Whatever faith doth please she may receive.
She may be Turk, Jew, Atheist, Infidel,
Or any thing, cause she need ne'er fear Hell,
215 For if she hath no Soul what need she fear
Something she knows not what or when or where.

But hold I think I should be silent now,
Because a Womans Soul you do allow.[73]
But had we none you'd say we had, else you
220 Could never damn us at the rate you do.
What dost thou think thou hast priviledge given,[74]
That those whom thou dost bless shall mount to
    heaven,
And those thou cursest unto hell must go.
And so dost think to fill the *Abiss* below
225 Quite full of Females, hoping there may be
No room for souls big with Vice as thee.[75]
But if that thou with such vain hopes should'st dye
I'th fluid Air,[76] thou must not think to fly,
Or enter into heaven, thy weight of Sin
230 Would crush the damn'd, and so thoud'st enter in.
But hold, I am uncharitable here,
Thou may'st repent, tho' that's a thing I fear.
But if thou should'st repent, why then again
It would at best but mitigate thy pain,
235 Because thou hast been vile to that degree,
That thy repentance must eternal be.
For wert thou guilty of no other crime
Than what thou lately puttest into Rhime,
Why that without other offences given,
240 Were enough to shut the gate of Heaven.[77]
But when together's put all thou do,[78]
It will not only shut but bar it too.

For when Heaven made woman it design'd[79]
Her for the charming object of Mankind.
245 Nor is alter'd only with those who

Set *Bewly*, *Stratford,* nay and *Chreswell* too,
Or other Bawds, chase their acquaintance out,
And then what they must be we make no doubt.[80]
'Tis to make heaven mistaken when you say
250 It meant one and it proves another way.
For when heaven with its last and greatest care,
Had form'd a female charming bright and fair,
Why then immediately it did decree,
That unto man she should a blessing be,
255 And so should prove to all posterity.
And surely there is nothing can be worse
Than for to turn a blessing to a curse.
And when the greatest blessing heaven ere gave,[81]
And certainly the best that man could have.[82]
260 When that's scorn'd and contemn'd[83] sure it must be
A great affront unto heaven's Majesty.
But I hope Heaven will punish the offence,
And with it justifie our Innocence.

I must confess there are some bad, and they
265 Lead by an *Ignis fatus,*[84] go astray:
All are not forc'd to wander in false way.
Only some few whose dark benighted sence,
For want of light han't power to make defence
Against those many tempting pleasures, which
270 Not only theirs but Masculine Souls bewitch.
But you'd persuade us, that 'tis we alone
Are guilty of all crimes and you have none,
Unless some few, which you call fools,[85] (who be
Espous'd to wives, and live in chastity.)
275 But the most rational without which we

Doubtless shou'd question your Humanity.[86]
And I would praise them more only I fear
If I should do't it would make me appear
Unto the World much fonder than I be
280 Of that same State,[87] for I love Liberty,
Nor do I think there's a necessity
For all to enter Beds, like *Noah*'s beast
Into his Ark; I would have some releast
From the dear cares of that lawful State:
285 Hold I'll not dictate, I'll leave all Fate.[88]
Nor would I have the World to think that I
Through a despair do *Nuptial Ioys* defy.
For in the World so little I have been
That I've but half a revolution seen
290 Of *Saturn*,[89] only I do think it best
For those who love to contemplate at rest,
For to live single too, and then they may
Uninterupted, *Natures Work* survey.
And had my Antagonist spent his time[90]
295 Making true Verse instead of spiteful Rhime,
As a Female Poet, he had gain'd some praise,
But now his malice blasts his twig of Bays.[91]
I do not wish you had,[92] for I believe
It is impossible for to deceive
300 Any with what you write, because that you
May insert things supposed true.[93]
And if by supposition I may go,
Then I'll suppose all men are wicked too,
Because I'm sure there's many that are so.
305 And 'cause you have made *Whores* of all you could,
So if you durst, you'd say all Women would.[94]

Which words do only argue guilt and spite:
All makes you cheap in ev'ry mortals sight.
And it doth shew that you have alwaies been
310 Only with Women guilty of that Sin.
You nere desired nor were you fit for those
Whose modest carriage doth their minds disclose.
And Sir, methinks you do describe so well
The way and manner *Bewley* enter'd Hell,[95]
315 As if your love for her had made you go
Down to the black infernal shades below.
But I suppose you never was so near,
For if you had, you scarce would have been here,
For had they seen, they'd kept you there.[96]
320 Unless they thought when ere it was you came,[97]
Your hot entrance[98] might encrease the flame.
If burning Hell add to their extreme pain,[99]
And so were glad to turn you off again.[100]
And likewise, also I believe beside,
325 That one thing more might be their haughty
        pride.[101]
They knew you Rival'd them in all their Crimes,
Wherewith they could debauch the willing times.
And as fond mortals[102] hate a rival, they
Loving through Pride,[103] were loath to let you stay,
330 For fear that you might their black deeds excel,
Usurp their Seat and be the Prince of Hell.
But I believe that you will let your hate
Ore rule your bride,[104] and you'll not wish the State
Of Governing, because your deceived mind,
335 Persuades your Subjects will be Women kind.[105]
But I believe when it comes the tryal,[106]

Ask but for ten and you'll have the denial.
You'd think your self far happier than you be,
Were you but half so sure of heaven as we.

340 But when you are in hell if you should find
More then I speak of,[107] think heaven design'd
Them for a part of your Eternal Fate,
Because they're things which you so much do hate.
But why you should do so I cannot tell,

345 Unless 'tis what makes you in love with hell:[108]
And having fallen-out with Goodness, you
Must have Antipathy 'gainst Woman too.
For virtue and they are so near ally'd
That none can their mutual tyes divide.[109]

350 Like Light and Heat, incorporate[110] they are,
And interwove with providential care,
But I'm too dull[111] to give my Sex due praise,
The task befits a Laureat Crown'd with Bays:[112]
And yet all he can say, will be but small,

355 A Copy differs from the original.
For should he sleep under *Parnassus* Hill,[113]
Implore the Muses for to guide his Quill.[114]
And shou'd they help him, yet his praise would seem
At best but undervalluing disesteem.[115]

360 For he would come so short of what they are
His lines won't with one single Act compare.[116]
But to say truest, is to say that she
Is Good and Virtuous unto that degree
As you pretend she's Bad, and that's beyond

365 Imagination, 'cause you set no bound,
And then one certain definition is
To say that she doth comprehend all Bliss.

And that she's all that's pious, chast and true,[117]
Heroick, constant, nay, and modest too:
370 The later Virtue is a thing you doubt,[118]
But 'tis 'cause you nere sought[119] to find it out.
You question where[120] there's such a thing or no,
'Tis only 'cause you hope you've lost a foe,[121]
A hated object, yet a stranger too.
375 I'll speak like you, if such a thing there be,[122]
I'm certain that she doth not dwell with thee.
Thou art Antipodes to that[123] and unto all
That's Good, or that we simply civil call.
From yokes of Goodness, thou'st thy self releast,[124]
380 Turn'd Bully Hector, and a humane Beast.[125]
That Beasts do speak it rarely comes to pass,
Yet you may paralell with *Balaam*'s Ass.[126]
You do describe a woman so that one
Would almost think she had the Fiends outdone:
385 As if at her strange birth did shine no star,
Or Planet, but Furies in conjunction were;
And did conspire what mischief they should do,
Each act his part[127] and her with plagues pursue,
'Tis false in her, yet 'tis sum'd up in you.[128]
390 You almost would perswade one that you thought[129]
That providence to a low ebb was brought;
And that to *Eve* and *Jezabell* was given
Souls of so great extent that heaven was driven
Into a Straight, and liberality
395 Had made her void of wanting, to supply
These later bodies,[130] she was forc'd to take
Their souls asunder, and so numbers make,
And transmigrate them into others, and

Still shift them as she finds the matters stand.
400 'Tis 'cause they are the worst makes me believe
You must imagine *Jezabel* and *Eve.*
But I'm no *Pythagorean*[131] to conclude
One Soul could serve for *Abraham* and *Jude.*[132]
Or think that heaven so bankrupt or so poor,
405 But that each body has one soul or more.
I do not find our Sex so near ally'd,
Either in disobedience or in pride,
Unto the 'bovenamed Females (for I'm sure
They are refin'd, or else were alwaies pure)
410 That I must needs conceit their souls the same,[133]
Tho' I confess there's some that merit blame:[134]
But yet their faults only thus much infer,
That we're not made so perfect but may err;[135]
Which adds much lustre to a virtuous mind,
415 And 'tis her prudence makes her soul confin'd
Within the bounds of Goodness, for if she
Was all perfection, unto that degree
That 'twas impossible to do amiss,
Why heaven not she must have the praise of this.
420 But she's in such a state as she may fall,
And without care her freedom may enthrall.
But to keep pure and free in such a case,
Argues each virtue with its proper grace.
And as a womans composition is
425 Most soft and gentle, she has happiness[136]
In that her soul is of that nature too,
And yeilds to any thing that heaven will do;
Takes an impression when 'tis seal'd in heaven,
Turns to a cold refusal, when 'tis given

430 By any other hand: She's all divine,
     And by a splendid lustre doth outshine
     All masculine souls, who only seem to be
     Made up of pride and their lov'd luxury.[137]
     So great's mans ambition that he would
435 Have all the wealth and power if he could,
     That is bestowed on the several Thrones
     Of the worlds Monarchs, covets all their Crowns.
     And by experience it hath been found
     The word Ambition's not an empty sound.
440 There's not an History which doth not shew
     Man's pride, ambition and his falshood too.
     For if at any time th'ambitious have
     Least shew of honour, then their souls grow brave,[138]
     Grow big and restless, they are not at ease,
445 'Till they have a more fatal way to please,
     Look fair and true, when falsely they intend;
     So from low Subject, grow a Monarch's Friend.
     And by grave Councels they their good pretend,
     When 'tis guilt poyson and oft works their end.[139]
450 The Son who must succeed, is too much loved,
     Must be pull'd down (his Councel is approved)
     For fear he willingly should grow too great,
     Desire to rule, should mount his father's Seat.
     So he's dispatch'd, and then all those that be
455 Next in the way are his adherency.[140]
     And then the better to secure the State,
     It is but just they should receive his fate.
     So by degrees he for himself makes room,
     His Prince is straightway shut up in his Tomb,
460 And then the false usurper mounts the Throne.[141]

Or would do so at least but commonly
He nere sits firm,[142] but with revenge doth dy,
But thank heaven there's but few that reach so high,
For the known crimes makes a wise Prince take care.
465 Thus what I've said doth plainly shew there are
Men more impious than a woman far.[143]
So those who by their abject fortune are
Remote from Courts no less their pride declare,
In being uneasie[144] and envying all who be
470 Above them, in State,[145] or Priority.
But 'tis impossible for to relate
Their boundless Pride, or their prodigious hate,
To all that fortune hath but smil'd upon,
In a degree that is above their own.[146]
475 And thou proud fool, that virtue would'st subdue,
Envying all good, dost towre ore woman too,
Which doth betray a base ignoble mind,
Speaks thee nothing but a blustring wind.[147]
But in so great a lab'rinth as man's pride,
480 I should not enter, nor won't be imply'd,[148]
For to search out their strange and unknown crimes,
There's so many apparent in these times,
That my dull Arithmetick cannot tell
Half the sins[149] that commonly do dwell
485 In one sordid Rustick,[150] then how can I
Define the Courts or Towns Debauchery.
Their pride in some small measure I have shown,
But theirs is running over and prest down;[151]
And 'tis impossible I should repeat
490 The Crimes of men extravagantly great,
I would not name them, but to let them see

I know they'r bad and odious unto me:
'Tis true, pride makes men great in their own eyes,
But them proportionable I despise;
495 And tho' Ambition still aims to be high,
Yet Lust at best is but beastiality;
A Sin with which there's none can compare,
Not Pride nor Envy, *&c.* for this doth insnare,[152]
Not only those whom it at first inflam'd,
500 This Sin must have a partner to be sham'd,
And punish'd like himself. Hold, one wont do,
He must have more, for he doth still pursue
The Agents of his Passion; 'tis not Wife,
That Mutual Name can regulate his Life:
505 And tho' he for his Lust might have a shrowd,
And there might be *Poligamy* allow'd,
Yet all his Wives would surely be abhorr'd,[153]
And some common *Lais* be ador'd.[154]
Most mortally the Name of Wife they hate,
510 Yet they will take one as their proper fate,
That they may have a Child legitimate,
To be their Heir, if they have an Estate,
Or else to bear their Names: So, for by ends,
They take a Wife,[155] and satisfie their friends,
515 Who are desirous that it should be so,
And for that end, perhaps, Estates bestow;
Which, when possess'd, is spent another way;
The Spurious Issue do the right betray,
And with their Mother-Strumpets are maintain'd;
520 The Wife and Children by neglect disdain'd,
Wretched and poor unto their Friends return,
Having got nothing, unless cause to mourn.

5. Illustration from printed broadside ballad, "A Statute for Swearers and Drunkards", dating from 1624.

The Dire Effects of Lust I cannot tell,
For I suppose its Catalogue's in Hell;
525 And he perhaps at last[156] may read it there,
Written in flames, fierce as his own whilst here.
I could say more,[157] but yet not half that's done
By these strange Creatures, nor is there scarce one
Of these inhumane Beasts that do not die[158]
530 As bad as *Bewley*'s Pox[159] turns Leprosie,
And Men do catch it by meer phantasie.[160]
Tho' they are chast and honest, yet it doth
Pursue them, and some company on oath
They have been in, and their infected breath
535 Gave them that Plague, which hast'neth their death,[161]
Or else 'tis Scurvy, or some new disease,
As the base wretch or vain Physician please,
And then a sum of Money must be gave
For to keep corruption from the grave;
540 And then 'tis doubled,[162] for to hide the cheat:
(O the sad Horrour of debaucht deceit!)
The Body and Estate together go.
And then the only Objects here below,
On which he doth his charity bestow,
545 Are Whores and Quacks, and perhaps Pages too
Must have a share, or else they will reveal
That which Money doth make them conceal.[163]
Sure trusty Stewards of extensive heaven,
When what's for common good is only given
550 Unto peculiar friends of theirs, who be
Slaves to their lust, friending debauchery;
These are partakers[164] of as great a fate
As those whose boldness turns them reprobate,

And tho' a Hypocrite doth seem to be
555 A greater sharer of Morality,
Yet methinks they almost seem all one,
One hides, and t'other tells what he hath done;
But if one Devil's better than another,
Than one of these is better than the t'other:[165]
560 Hypocrisie preheminence should have,[166]
(Tho' it ha'nt got the priviledge to save)
Because the Reprobate's example may,
By open Custom, make the rugged way
Seem more smooth, and a common sin
565 Look more pardonable,[167] and so by him
More take example, 'tis he strives to win.
Mad Souls, to fill up Hell! But should there be[168]
Nothing e're acted but Hypocrisie,[169]
Yet Man would be as wicked as he is,
570 And be no nearer to eternal bliss;
For he who's so unsteady, as to take
Example by such Men, should never make
Me to believe, that he was really chast,
And, without pattern, never had imbrac't:[170]
575 Such kind of sins at best such virtues weak,
That with such a slender stress will break,[171]
And that's no virtue which cannot withstand
A slight temptation at the second hand:
But I believe one might as narrowly pry
580 For't, as the *Grecian*[172] did for honesty,
And yet find none; and then if Women be
Averse to't too, sure all's iniquity
On this side Heaven, and it with Justice went
Up thither,[173] 'cause here is found no content,

585 But did regardless and neglected ly,
  And with an awful distance was past by.[174]
  Instead of hiding their prodigious Acts,
  They do reveal, brag of their horrid Facts;[175]
  Unless it be some few who hide them, 'cause
590 They would not seem to violate those laws
  Which with their tongues they'r forc'd for to
    maintain,
  Being grave Counsellers or Aldermen,
  Or else the Wives Relations are alive,
  And then, if known, some other way they'l drive
595 Their golden wheels,[176] that way doth seem uneven,
  Then the Estate most certainly is given
  Some other way, or else 'tis setled so
  As he may never have it to bestow,
  Upon his Lusts,[177] therefore he doth seem
600 For to have a very great esteem
  For his pretended Joy; but when her friends
  Are dead, then he his cursed life defends,
  With what they leave; then the unhappy wife,
  With her dear children, lead an horrid life,
605 And the Estate's put to another use,
  And their great kindness turn'd an abuse;[178]
  And should I strive their falshood to relate,
  Then I should have but *Sisiphus* his fate,[179]
  For Man is so inconstant and untrue,
610 He's like a shadow which one doth pursue,
  Still flies from's word, nay and perfidious too.
  An Instance too of Infidelity[180]
  We have in *Egypt*'s false King *Ptolomy*,[181]
  Who, tho' he under obligations were,

615 For to protect *Pompey* from the snare,
Who fled to him for succour, yet base he
Did command his death most treacherously;
He was inconstant too, or else design'd
The same at first, so alter'd words not mind,[182]
620 Which is much worse, for when that one doth
 speak
With a full resolution, for to break[183]
One's word and oath, surely it must be
A greater crime than an inconstancy,
Which is as great failing in the soul[184]
625 As any sin that reason doth controul,
But I designed for to be short, so must
Be sure for to keep firm unto the first
That I resolved, or else should reprove
These faults which first I ought for to remove;[185]
630 Therefore, with *Brutus*, I this point will end,
Who, tho' he ought to have been *Cæsar*'s
 friend,[186]
By being declared his Heir, yet it was he
Was the first actor in his tragedy:
Perfidious and ungrateful and untrue
635 He was at once, nay and disloyal too:[187]
A thousand Instances there might be brought,
(Not far fetch'd, tho' they were dearly bought)
To prove that Man more false than Woman is,
More unconstant, nay and more perfidious:[188]
640 But these are Crimes which hell, (I'm sure not
 heaven)
As they pretend, hath peculiar given
Unto our Sex, but 'tis as false as they,[189]

And that's more false than any one can say.
All Pride and Lust too to our charge they lay,
645 As if in sin we all were so sublime
As to monopolize each hainous crime;
Nay, Woman now is made the Scape-goat, and
'Tis she must bear sins of all the land:[190]
But I believe there's not a Priest that can
650 Make an atonement for one single man,
Nay, it is well if he himself[191] can bring
An humble, pious heart for th'offering;
A thing which ought to be inseparable
To men o'th' Gown[192] and of the Sacred Table;
655 Yet it is sometimes wanting, and they be
Too often sharers of Impiety:
But howsoever the strange World now thrives,
I must not look in my Teachers lives,[193]
But methinks the World doth seem to be
660 Nought but confusion and degeneracy,
Each Man's so eager of each fatal sin,
As if he fear'd he should not do't again;
Yet still his soul is black, he is the same
At all times, tho' he doth not act all flame,
665 Because he opportunity doth want,
And to him always there's not a grant
Of Objects[194] for to exercise his will,
And for to shew his great and mighty skill
In all Sciences diabolical,
670 But when he meets with those which we do call
Base and unjust, why then his part he acts
Most willingly, and then with hell contracts
To do the next thing that they should require;

6. *"Recipe for Marital Bliss"* (c. 1680), German woodcut
attributed to Abraham Bach of Augsburg.

And being thus inflamed with hellish fire,
675 He doth to any thing it doth desire,[195]
Unless 'twere possible for hell to say,
They should be good, for then they'd disobey.[196]
I am not sorry you do Females hate,[197]
But rather reckon we're more fortunate,
680 Because I find, when you'r right understood,
You are at enmity with all that's good,[198]
And should you love them, I should think they were
A growing bad, but still keep as you are:
I need not bid you, for you must I'm sure,
685 And in your present wretched state indure;
'Tis an impossible[199] you should be true,
As for a Woman to act like to you,

Which I am sure will not accomplish'd be,
Till heaven's turn'd hell, and that's
    repugnancy;[200]
690 And when vice is virtue you shall have
A share of that which makes most Females
    brave,[201]
Which transmutations I am sure can't be;
So thou must lie in vast eternity,[202]
With prospect of thy endless misery,
695 When Woman, your imagin'd Fiend,[203] shall live
Bless'd with the Joys that Heaven can always give.

FINIS.

EXPLANATORY NOTES

In what follows, the title of Egerton's *Female Advocate* is abbreviated as *FA*; and the title of the satire which it is answering, *Love given o're*, is abbreviated as *LGO*.

Although points of pronunciation are in most instances beyond the scope of these notes, the rhymes in *FA* are far better appreciated if the differences between today's vowel sounds and those known to Egerton are borne in mind. In his *Accents of English: An Introduction*, 3 vols (Cambridge: Cambridge University Press, 1982), 1: 196, J. C. Wells observes, for instance, that "break" and "great" are among the words whose "pronunciation fluctuated in the eighteenth century between /i:/ (FLEECE) and /e:/ (FACE)"; as late as 1772, he adds, the pronunciation of "great" was still not fixed and there was a powerful lobby for the vowel sound in it to be put on a par with that in "seat". A couplet like "For fear he willingly should grow too great,/ Desire to rule, should mount his father's Seat" (lines 452-3) therefore makes a perfectly satisfactory rhyme. Egerton also rhymes "great" with "compleat" (lines 15-16) and with "repeat" (lines 489-90), while she rhymes "break" with "weak" (lines 575-6) and with "speak" (lines 620-21).

1. **my *Virgin-Modesty* hath put:** Egerton would later revise this (1687), so that the wording ran "an intelligent Modesty informs my Soul, I ought to put" and therefore represented her as having acted out of discretion rather than diffidence.

2. **condemn me for a *Talkative*:** Talkativeness, according to Richard Allestree in Section VI of his *Government of the Tongue* (1674), is what "we used to call ... a Feminine vice"; but really there is no reason, he says, to "appropriate Loquacity to Women". In John Bunyan's *Pilgrim's Progress* (1678–84) Talkative is a male character. However, the stereotype persisted. See Hardy, "The Talkative Woman in Shakespeare, Dickens and George Eliot", 15-45.

3. **the Importunities of her obliging Friends:** Pressure to publish is seen as coming from those whose eagerness to please the author makes them perhaps too prompt in praising her. Grammatically, the sentence requires "their" and not "her".

4. **what it was put me upon the Publication of this:** Before "put me", "that" or "which" is understood. Elaine Hobby points out that Egerton later made a crucial change to her story, stating in her preface to the 1687 edition that she "could not hinder" publication of the 1686 edition (Hobby 144).

5. **the Debauchery which I now answer, is a sufficient warrant for this appearing of mine:** Egerton means that her justification for making a public show of herself is the perverted and perverting nature of the work, Gould's poem *Love given o're*, which has stung her into doing so. When revised (1687) her preface no longer termed this work a "Debauchery"—though it still plainly went "beyond the bounds of Modesty and Civility"—because Egerton was aware that in a new edition it had been toned down somewhat.

6. **he doth not only exclaim … Honesty too:** The "he" is, so far as Egerton is concerned, unidentifiable; *LGO* having been published anonymously, she could not have known that the author's name was Robert Gould.

7. **those who pretend to be the most perfect and rational Creatures:** Both here and in line 641 of the poem proper, to "pretend" is not so much to play-act as to make a false claim.

8. **if they are of the right Church they shall be infallibly saved:** Among the sects which had flourished during the period of the Civil War and the Commonwealth (1642–60) were some subscribing to the antinomian view that those supposedly singled out for God's grace were elected to heaven whether or not they followed Christian moral teaching ("the Rules which lead to Salvation", or Heaven's "Law").

9. **pass currant in Heaven:** i.e., "are accepted in heaven", as if they were legal tender there. "Inscription" (the wording on a coin) sets up this metaphor.

10. **seem to have the Claim:** Presumably not wishing to be thought to have meant "sole claim", Egerton later altered this to "seem to have the justest Claim" (1687).

11. **Blasphemous Wretch, who canst:** The Chawton House and British Library copies of the 1686 edition carry ink corrections (presumably the printer's) turning "who canst" into "thou who canst". Egerton's subsequent preference (1687) was "Blasphemous Wretch! How canst thou …".

12. **usurp't the way:** later corrected to "Usurpt the Sway" (1687).
13. **Gods Omniscience and Omnipresence too:** This line fitted more satisfyingly into the poem's metrical system when for the 1687 edition (in one of many adjustments then made to the text for the sake of rhythmic regularity) it was turned around to read "God's Omnipresence and Omniscience too" (1687).
14. **Degenerate Man utter Blasphemy:** metrically adjusted in 1687 to read "Degen'rate Man speak such vile Blasphemy".
15. **Made all things glorious it did undertake:** "And" is understood before "made", and "which" is understood after "glorious".
16. **freely plac'd:** In the British Library copy of the 1686 edition (though not in the Chawton House copy), the "d" of "plac'd" is inked out and a "t" substituted, in order—one supposes—to emphasise the rhyme with "taste".
17. **All things pleasant:** metrically adjusted in 1687 to read "Each thing that's pleasant".
18. **consummate all Bliss:** a claim repeated, with variation, in line 367 ("comprehend all Bliss").
19. **'twas not fit for Man to be alone:** Egerton draws here on Genesis 2.18 (in the Authorized Version, "And the Lord God said, It is not good that the man should be alone").
20. **that of Man's:** Despite the two colliding possessive constructions, this wording is retained in both the 1687 and 1707 editions.
21. **banish'd Truth for spight:** Truth and spite are opposites throughout *FA* (see line 295); and, as Egerton's "Antagonist", Robert Gould is the epitome of the latter (see line 92).
22. **quite so guilty as some make:** i.e., "make out".
23. **from God's own Mouth had the Command:** The "Command" is the one handed down to Adam in Genesis 2.16-17, the ban on eating of the tree of the knowledge of good and evil.
24. *Eve* **had the … least Charge:** In other words, the burden of blame borne by Eve was (or should have been) less heavy.
25. **But though Woman Man to Sin did lead:** The 1687 text changes "though" to "tho' that" for the sake of the metre—the two conjunctions combined having the same force as the first alone—and at the end of the line it replaces with a comma the 1686 punctuation, a question-mark in italic type. (Since this question-mark is unaccountable and apparently erroneous, it is omitted from the text as reproduced here.)
26. **her Seed hath bruis'd the Serpent's Head:** After tempting Eve in the Garden of Eden, the serpent is told that "her seed … shall bruise thy head" (Genesis 3.15).

27. **still their greatest haters:** "Still" has the force of "always" here.

28. **For they associate ... their Debauchery:** These four lines, implying licentious behaviour on the part of Egerton's "Antagonist", were suppressed after 1686; they do not appear in the editions of 1687 and 1707.

29. **They make all base for ones Immodesty:** Egerton's 1687 preface returns to this theme. "When a Man is so extravagant as to Damn all Womankind for the Crimes of a few", she writes, "he ought to be corrected".

30. **make the Name:** The name (which the "haters" consider a curse, but which Egerton will of course construe as "a Charm") is that of woman.

31. **censure married Men to Hell:** "Censure" is later replaced by "conjure" (1687), which co-operates better with "Magick Spell" in the previous line.

32. **your's is a Fire ... :** Directly addressing her opponent, Egerton tells him that his inspiration comes from the powers of darkness, who are angry with women for doing so little to swell the population of hell.

33. **if so universally they are:** The "are" at the end of the line would in Egerton's day have been sounded like "air", which (not only here but in lines 465, 467, and 683) creates some unexpected rhyming possibilities. Christopher Cooper's *The English Teacher* (1687) documents this pronunciation. It is still thought proper by Joe Gargery in Dickens's *Great Expectations* (1860–61), who on visiting Pip in London greets him with "how AIR you, Pip?"

34. **With each approaching Morn a Prodigy:** Egerton as Female Advocate continues her cross-examination of the author of *LGO* by completing a question, begun in the previous couplet, which seeks to trap him in an illogicality. If he were right about women, she argues, their moral monstrosity would (on a daily basis) be so apparent as to render quite unnecessary his labour in detailing their "Pride, Lust, and Inconstancy, &c.".

35. **Man curse dead woman; I could hear as well:** "Dead" is later changed to "bad" (1687), which fits far better with Egerton's endeavour to establish the blindness of men to the beams in their own eyes. At the same time, and inexplicably, the 1687 text alters "hear" to "here"; but the 1707 text restores "hear".

36. **there had been no such place:** "Had been" carries a conditional sense: "would have been". "No such place" is later expanded into "no such damn'd Place" (1687), in order to fill out the line as the metre requires.

37. **Make some chaste Wives to merit a Divorce:** The full stop at the end of this line is misleading—and is replaced in 1687 and 1707 by a colon—since the sense is continuous; this passage suggests that the author of *LGO* has caused petitions to be brought down upon the heads of perfectly blameless women merely (Egerton's "but") because they saw his wicked lust for what it was.

38. **adulterate all Womankind:** "Adulterate" in this context means to debauch, which is exactly what a campaign like the one Egerton imagines the author of *LGO* to have launched against "all the Females in [his] way" threatens to accomplish.

39. **rob *Hymen* of his Deity:** cast out the (Greek) god of marriage—and so condemn themselves once more to living alone, "A barren Sex, and insignificant" (line 19).

40. **They would be glad to keep their Men ... :** With no more children being born, there would soon be too few men to go round, either as household retainers or (when this thought is pursued into lines 104-7) as courtiers.

41. **keep the number of's Nobility:** "Keep" has the sense of "keep up", or prevent from declining. (In order for numbers to be kept up, however, Egerton ventures the suggestion that before long every man remaining would have to be co-opted into the peerage.) One of the obvious 1686 misprints, which had the line reading "would keep the number of of's Nobility", has been corrected here.

42. **a Kingdom cramb'd into a Court:** either "crammed" (to show the court as filled to bursting) or "cramped" (to suggest a diminished and devalued kingdom). In 1687 the "b" is removed, leaving "cram'd"; but the 1686 text is possibly influenced by Andrew Marvell's "cramped into a planisphere", from his poem "The Definition of Love" (published 1681).

43. **a Baudy House or Nunnery:** These are the only two obvious options for women which are left, Egerton suggests, after marriage is ruled out. The latter is the one that women would surely pick, she says, once marriage had been legally abolished.

44. **Or should this Act ere pass:** In the second edition of *FA* (1687), this line was improved by the insertion of "For" in place of "or" and the substitution of "e'er" for "ere".

45. **before their lovers flames:** i.e., rather than submit to the lust of those who (in the sense which was operative in line 85) "courted" them.

46. **The chast *Lucretia* ... Her he slew:** The revised text of 1687, "Her self she slew", removes an error. Tarquin violated Lucretia but did not kill her; rather, as her only means of wiping away what in Shakespeare's poem on the subject she terms "this forced stain", she chose suicide. Among the painters inspired by Lucretia's tragic story were Titian and, as is of course attested by Illustration number 3, Rembrandt.

47. **Witness those *Saxon* Ladies ... :** Egerton refers to the ninth-century abbess of Coldingham, the martyred St Ebba, who cut off her nose and upper lip—and directed all of her nuns to do likewise—in order that they might seem hideous to the marauding Danes. All of the "Ladies" were then burned alive, as "their sacrifices", by the Danes whom they had thwarted.

48. **curst *Osbright* courted *Beon's* wife:** This is another story from the ninth century. Osbright was the King of Northumberland, and Holinshed's *Chronicles* have him "ravish[ing]" the wife of Beon (or "Berne"). The Danes, to whose king the victim was related, settled the score by killing Osbright. Both the couplet about "curst Osbright" and the next two lines, whose vague allegations could have caused trouble and embarrassment, were removed from the 1687 and 1707 editions.

49. **In Constancy they men excell as far ...:** This and the next five lines (i.e., lines 137-142) are extensively recast in 1687; and the changes add tenacity to Egerton's argument, although they also make the passage's repetition of the previous line's rhyme-word—"excel"—even more jarring. The revised and expanded version reads as follows:

> In Constancy they often Men excel,
> That steady Vertue in their Souls do dwell;
> She's not so fickle and frail as Men pretend,
> But can keep constant to a faithful Friend;
> And tho' Man's always alt'ring of his mind,
> He says, Inconstancy's in Womankind;
> And would persuade us that we engross all
> That's either fickle, vain or whimsical.
> Man's fancy'd Truth small Vertue doth express;
> Our's is Constancy, their's is Stubbornness.
> In faithful Love our Sex do them out-shine,
> And is more constant than the Masculine ...

Egerton's "out-shine" is a like-for-like replacement for the overworked "excel[l]", which throughout the poem (not just here but in lines 83 and 330) she uses transitively, to mean "exceed" or "surpass".

50. **A heavens bright lamp:** The compositor has presumably missed the "s" of "As" here, and the construction of Egerton's comparison—women eclipsing men as emphatically as the sun outshines a pale star—is consequently obscured.

51. **Inconstancy is only in womankind:** Egerton does not of course mean that this is literally the case—although *Love given o're* had claimed it was: "constant onely in Inconstancy" (*LGO* 11)—but rather that men cunningly make it appear to be so.

52. **no hold, it isn't:** On reflection, Egerton suggests, it is no wonder that women are so often deemed to fall short; for men see to it that far more is demanded of women in terms of constancy than would ever be expected from men.

53. **Or ere expired with his loving Bride:** This line was later rewritten (1687), with "ever suffer'd" replacing "ere expired" and a question-mark substituted for the concluding full stop.

54. **tho in flames of fire:** The editions of 1687 and 1707 are a little more lurid here: "wrapt in flaming fire".

55. **this is done by *Indian* women:** The Hindu practice of *suttee* (widows submitting to be burned on their husbands' funeral pyres) was known about, though not under that name, in the late seventeenth century. The closing moments of John Dryden's play *Aureng-Zebe* (1675) highlight the peculiar predicament of "*Indian* Wives": "fatally their Virtue they approve;/ Chearful in Flames, and Martyrs of their Love".

56. **More glorious *Phoenix* than the *Arabian* fields:** The phoenix was a mythical Arabian bird which lived for five hundred years and then set itself on fire so that a new phoenix could rise from the ashes.

57. **The *German* women Constancy did shew:** The legend of the faithful wives of Weinsberg revolves around a twelfth-century siege, in the course of which a promise of safe passage was made for the women in the garrison and whatever valuables they were able to carry; they then emerged, as shown in Illustration number 4, bearing their menfolk on their backs and proclaiming that—with their worldly goods all abandoned to the besieging force—these were the valuables they had chosen to take out with them.

58. **Drownded in tears by their cold husbands side:** This of course counters the story of the Ephesian Matron (as discussed in the Introduction) who "made a Brothel of her Husband's Tomb".

59. **And when a Sword … void of breath:** These four lines were omitted in 1687 and 1707.

60. **why then the Sun/ With Constant Motion don't his progress run:** This comparison, though less careful astronomically than in the revised text of 1687 ("why then the Sun/ Or Earth do not a constant progress run"), invests the loving wives whose virtues Egerton has been celebrating with the same quality of unfailing devotion which is captured in the Morning Hymn of Thomas Ken (1637–1711): "Awake, my soul, and with the sun/ Thy daily course of duty run …".

61. **But when she's courted … the reason's just:** These two lines were in 1687 made into four:

    But when to us pretended Love is made,
    We yielding, find it Lust in Masquerade:
    Then we disown it, Vertue says we must,
    We well may change, I think the reason just.

62. **No, she bright Star … :** Woman is figured here as a lodestar—symbolising steadfastness because it appears always to occupy the same position in the heavens, and far brighter than the "dull twinckling star" (line 138) associated with the male sex. The serene stability of the North Star, seeming to remain firm while all beneath her wanders, is celebrated in two famous sonnets, Shakespeare's "Let me not to the marriage of true minds" ("Love is … the star to every wand'ring bark") and "Bright star! Would I were steadfast as thou art" by John Keats (1795–1821).

63. **joyn with an insatiate love:** At least in respect of the author of *Love given o're*, Egerton has already (in line 89) established insatiable desire as an ingredient not in female but in masculine souls. She turns the tables on Gould by applying to him an epithet which he had reserved for the excesses of women as notorious as "*Rome*'s Emperial Whore" or "Our late illustrious *Bewley*" (*LGO* 3-4).

64. **whose first espoused to vertue:** "Whose" requires to be read as "who's"; any confusion, however, is later prevented (1687) by its emendation to "that's".

65. **now the scene is alter'd … :** Egerton means that *Love given o're* has created such a climate of slander and suspicion that even the most demure of women may now be perceived and portrayed as a shameless hussy.

66. **Worse than mock-verse doth the most solid Play:** One example of what Egerton might have in mind here would be the burlesque comedy *The Rehearsal* (1672), by George Villiers, Duke of Buckingham. That play's travesty of the heroic tragedies of the day pales, she suggests, beside what *Love given o're* has done to traduce women.

67. **bred up in *Venus* School:** i.e., taught to behave licentiously. A notorious pornographic work of this period was in fact entitled *The School of Venus*. Published in 1680, it was an anonymous translation of the French work *L'Ecole des filles* (1655), attributed to Michel Millot.

68. **straight is taxt with ungentility:** i.e., is immediately accused of unsophisticated thinking.

69. **Unless it be the little blinded Boy:** i.e., unless her "Deity" (line 188) is Cupid, god of Love. (Cupid was said to have no eyes because—according to Silvestris in Act 4 Scene 1 of John Lyly's play *Love's Metamorphosis*, first performed around 1590—"he hits he knows not whom"; and his mother, Venus, was "daughter to the Sea" in the sense of having risen from it.) Egerton goes on to argue, however, that those who profess devotion to Cupid do so only as a pretext to cover their lust; they have little knowledge of, or time for, true love.

70. **do invocate him:** The hypermetric "do" was dropped from the editions of 1687 and 1707.

71. **believe without controul ... a Woman had no Soul:** i.e., accept entirely unchallenged the old view that women have no souls. There is, however, no basis for supposing that this ever formed part of Christian teaching. See Nolan, "The Mysterious Affair at Mâcon: The Bishops and the Souls of Women", 501-507.

72. **no obligation ... to act what may be just or wise:** Egerton's prefatory address "To the Reader" has already suggested the horror with which she regards those convinced that they need "never follow the Rules which lead to Salvation".

73. **But hold ... a Womans Soul you do allow:** Acknowledging that her opponent (whom she again directly addresses) is not in fact among those who would deny women souls, Egerton refers back to lines 205-6. However, while "hold" in line 206 meant "assert" or "maintain", the "hold" which is introduced here—as also in lines 141, 231, and 285—is Egerton's rhetorical command to herself to pause, creating an aposiopesis. She thus appropriates one of her opponent's favourite devices: "But hold ... But hold ... But stop my Pen ... But stay" (*LGO* 6, 11, 12.)

74. **What dost thou think thou hast priviledge given:** This is a rather elliptical line, in which (despite the absence of any punctuation) the "What" is asked to stand on its own as an exclamation; and "hast priviledge given", with its succeeding "That ...", needs to be understood as "have a (or the) priviledge given to you ...". In the 1687 and 1707 editions, accordingly, "What" is comma'd off and "priviledge" comes with an indefinite article.

75. **souls big with Vice as thee:** Egerton later added, or restored, the word that the metre requires: "souls as big with Vice as thee ..." (1687).

76. **I'th fluid air:** René Descartes (1596–1650) and Robert Boyle (1627–1691) had contributed influentially to the current understanding of space, and air, as filled with subtle fluid. The 1687 text ("I'th' fluid Air") adds the expected eliding apostrophe.

77. **Were enough to shut the gate of Heaven:** "Were enough" was metrically adjusted in 1687 to read "were crime enough". The "were" carries a conditional sense: "would be".

78. **But when together's put all thou do:** The 1687 reading, "But, put together all that thou dost do", is more satisfying metrically, and the sense is also made clearer by the inserted "that".

79. **For when Heaven made woman it design'd ... :** This and the following twenty lines, up to and including line 263, are radically rethought in the 1687 edition. Only six of the original twenty-one are retained, while twelve entirely new lines are blended in, to produce a passage which no longer names names and whose main expressive weight has been transferred to its abstract nouns. It runs as follows:

> When wise Heav'n made Woman, it design'd
> Her for the charming object of Mankind:
> And surely Man degen'rate must be,
> That doth deny our Native purity.
> Nor is there scarce a thing that can be worse,
> Than turning of a Blessing to a curse.
> 'Tis to make Heav'n mistaken when you say
> It meant, at first, what proves another way:
> For Woman was created good, and she
> Was thought the best of frail Mortality:
> An help for man, his greatest good on Earth,
> Made for to sympathize his Grief and Mirth;
> Then why should man pretend she's worse than hell,
> The only plague ot'h [sic] world, and in her dwell
> All that is base or ill; no, she's not so,
> Rather she is the greatest good below;
> Most real virtue and true happiness,
> His only steady and most constant bliss.

80. **Nor is alter'd ... we make no doubt:** The names of Betty Buly (see note 63), Sarah Stratford, and Madam Cresswell were at this time well known around the brothels of London. All

three are cited in *LGO* (4-5) as having encouraged "Lusts Enthusiastick Rage", and all three are similarly alluded to in other satirical writing both before and after. See Wilson, *Court Satires of the Restoration*, 223. The lines discussing them in *FA*—perhaps, in an attempt to take out the most actionable phrases, mangled by some hand other than Egerton's own—are so knotty as to resist all untying except through conjectural emendation, but the general sense is clear: although these women move in exceptionally disreputable circles, even the most glaring exceptions cannot suffice to disprove the rule, that woman is the epitome of what is "charming bright and fair".

81. **the greatest blessing heaven ere gave:** We know from the 1687 emendations of lines 112 and 144 (see notes 44 and 53) that the "ere" in those lines was intended to be an "e'er" or "ever"; and the same presumably applies here.

82. **And certainly the best that man could have:** The punctuation that Egerton intended at the end of this line was a comma, we might assume, rather than a full stop.

83. **contemn'd:** not a misprint for "condemned", but a separate word meaning "despised" or "treated with contempt".

84. **Lead by an *Ignis fatus*:** i.e., misled as if by a will-o'-the-wisp. The Latin term is "ignis fatuus" (not "ignis fatus"), and the literal meaning is "foolish fire". Andrew Marvell's poem "The Mower to the Glowworms" (published 1681) refers to wandering mowers that "after foolish fires do stray".

85. **some few, which you call fools:** To marry, and settle contentedly to a life of monogamy, counts in *Love given o're* as criminal folly; in its closing lines the poem warns its readers not to be "so mad, so resolutely vain", as to venture "on the wild, rocky, matrimonial Sea". He who dares simply shows himself a "Sot", the poem says, and fit to be classified as "frenzical" (*LGO* 12).

86. **But the most rational ... :** "Yet far from being the most foolish of men", Egerton's couplet might be paraphrased as saying, "these are actually the most sensible; and but for them we women would take a very dim view of the male sex generally."

87. **that same State:** i.e., the married state.

88. **Hold I'll not dictate, I'll leave all Fate:** later revised to "But I'll not dictate, I'll leave all to Fate" (1687).

89. **Nor would I have the World ... *Saturn*:** Egerton assures her readers that, if she seems lukewarm about marriage, this does not (yet) come of bitter personal experience; for she is, or at the

time of writing *was*, only around fourteen years old. (Saturn was thought to complete its orbit of the sun in twenty-eight years—a slight underestimate of its actual period of revolution.) Egerton's *Poems* of 1703 claim even more about the age (and the speed) at which she composed *FA*: "Scarce fourteen Years, when I the piece begun,/ And in less time than fourteen days 'twas done" (quoted in Medoff 156 and Smith 182). However, the original protestation (lines 286-90 above) was removed from the 1687 and 1707 editions of *FA* itself. Line 290, with its opening torn away, was then rebuilt so that it read "Yet do I think a single life is best", with the potential repetition of "single life"/ "live single" averted by line 292 becoming "For then they're free from trifling Toys, and may".

90. **And had my Antagonist spent his time:** metrically adjusted in 1687 to read, "Had my Antagonist but spent his time".

91. **his twig of Bays:** A garland of bay-tree leaves (and twigs) was the traditional prize for poetic achievement.

92. **I do not wish you had … many that are so:** The seven lines which begin here might be paraphrased as follows: "Your malicious poem cannot in fact damage truth because anyone can see how absurd it is to argue from the individual specimen to the whole set (or in other words, as in line 65, to 'make all base for ones Immodesty'); I, using the same tactic, could just as easily fire off a wholesale condemnation of men."

93. **May insert things supposed true:** As it stands, this is a bungled line—at variance with the poem's metre, and failing to give to "supposed" the degree of emphasis which it really requires. The line was later altered to "Do only insert things supposed true" (1687).

94. **if you durst, you'd say all Women would:** "If you durst" means "if you dared", and "would turn to whoring"—that is, turn to the "Sin" of line 310—is understood at the end of the line. (The title of George Etherege's 1668 comedy *She Wou'd If She Cou'd* employs a similarly suggestive elision.) Once again Egerton is throwing a comment of her opponent's back in his face: "if they durst, all Women wou'd be Whores" (*LGO* 5).

95. **you do describe so well/ The way and manner *Bewley* enter'd Hell:** Egerton refers to a particularly colourful passage—including such details as "The murm'ring Fiends all hover'd round about,/ And in hoarse howls did the great Bawd salute"—in *LGO* (4-5).

96. **had they seen, they'd kept you there:** The reader is left to guess what or who are designated by the pronoun "they"—

presumably, up to and including line 331, the same "black infernal Devils" that were mentioned earlier (line 80). So it is by them that Egerton's opponent would have been kept in hell.

97. **when ere it was you came:** "When ere" was subsequently printed as "whene'er" (1687).

98. **Your hot entrance:** In the 1687 edition this is altered to "Your red-hot entrance" (and the unwanted full stop at the end of the line disappears).

99. **If burning Hell add to their extreme pain:** This line, which is not part of the devils' sequence of thought, is parenthesised in the 1687 and 1707 editions.

100. **turn you off again:** "Turn ... off" has the sense of "turn away".

101. **And likewise, also ... pride:** This couplet, one of Egerton's loosest, was improved by revision: "There's one thing more I do believe beside/ Might be occasion'd by their haughty Pride" (1687).

102. **fond mortals:** i.e., men in love.

103. **Loving through Pride:** The apparent misprint in this line was later corrected: "Loving their Pride" (1687).

104. **Ore rule your bride:** Corrected in 1687 to "O'er-rule your Pride", this is the sort of transcription error to which Egerton's "they ... writ what they pleas'd" (see Note on the Text) presumably refers.

105. **you'll not wish the State ... Women kind:** The devils' fears of being dominated and outdone would in fact prove groundless, Egerton suggests, since her opponent would be deterred from ever attempting to reign in hell by his own deluded notion that such reigning must necessarily be over a monstrous regiment of women. (Printed as two words, "Women kind" may of course mislead; the 1687 edition accordingly has "Womenkind".)

106. **when it comes the tryal:** That is, when you visit hell and put your theory to the test you won't be able to find even ten women there; for wicked women are rare indeed. "When it comes the tryal" was altered in 1687 to "whenever comes the tryal".

107. **More then I speak of:** in other words, more than ten. (Modern "than" is often written or printed as "then" in the seventeenth century.)

108. **Unless 'tis what makes you in love with hell:** i.e., unless it comes from the same wicked perversity which accounts for your strong attraction to hell itself.

109. **For virtue and they ... mutual tyes divide:** Egerton is attempting to match a famous couplet of John Dryden's, from his 1681 poem *Absalom and Achitophel*: "Great Wits are sure to

Madness near ally'd;/ And thin Partitions do their Bounds divide" (lines 163-4). The revised 1687 version of Egerton's lines brings them closer to the sharpness of Dryden's original: "For virtue and they so nearly are ally'd/ That none their mutual tyes can e'er divide."

110. **Like Light and Heat, incorporate:** Light and heat are most obviously "incorporate" (or, as the next line has it, "interwove") in the sun, with which women's defining virtue of constancy has already been strongly associated (see note 60 on lines 168-9).

111. **too dull:** i.e., too slow-witted, too much of a dullard. (Compare line 483, "my dull Arithmetick".)

112. **a Laureat Crown'd with Bays:** On the bays, see note 91 on line 297. John Dryden, to whom Egerton would later pay tribute in an ode (see Medoff 170), had been appointed Poet Laureate in 1668. He lived from 1631 to 1700.

113. **should he sleep under *Parnassus* Hill:** i.e., even if he were to frequent the mountain of the Muses themselves, and fetch his inspiration from there.

114. **guide his Quill:** A comma rather than a full stop is needed at the end of this line, since the sense is continuous. The requisite adjustment was duly made in 1687.

115. **his praise ... undervalluing disesteem:** His praise would be such a pale imitation (or "Copy") of the glorious reality, Egerton says, that it could only amount to insulting disparagement.

116. **His lines won't with one single Act compare:** Continuing the hyperbole, Egerton states that their (women's) slightest deed would make his (the laureate's) words seem hopelessly inadequate.

117. **she's all that's pious, chast and true:** These words are at the furthest possible remove from those which in the 1687 text Egerton puts into her opponent's mouth, about women "engross[ing] all/ That's either fickle, vain or whimsical" (see note 49 on line 137).

118. **The later Virtue is a thing you doubt:** "Later" meaning "latter" occurs both here and in line 396, although the correction made there (see note 130) was never in fact made here.

119. **you nere sought:** "Nere" is in the next edition (1687) replaced by "ne'er".

120. **You question where:** "Where", by the same token, is really "whe'er" (for "whether")—but could be left unaltered in both the 1687 and 1707 editions because "where" was commonly recognised as a dialectal contraction of "whether".

121. **you hope you've lost a foe:** According to Egerton's analysis, the doubt which the satire she has set herself to answer casts upon the existence of modesty in women—"Woman, in whose Breasts thou'rt said to raign,/ ... Despises thee, and only courts the Name" (*LGO* 6)—is merely a man's wishful thinking; by denying female modesty he disposes of an obvious obstacle to his lust.

122. **I'll speak like you, if such a thing there be:** Egerton is indeed directly quoting her opponent's words on (female) modesty: "'tis a doubt if such a thing there be" (*LGO* 6).

123. **Thou art Antipodes to that:** i.e., you are diametrically opposed to everything modest. In *The Fall of Hyperion* (1.199-200) John Keats has the lines "The poet and the dreamer are distinct,/ Diverse, sheer opposite, antipodes."

124. **From yokes of Goodness, thou'st thy self release:** The awkward contraction was later written out of the line: "From Vertue's yoke thou hast thy self release" (1687).

125. **Turn'd Bully Hector, and a humane Beast:** The textual changes of 1687 and 1707 serve to improve a line which already alliterates neatly around its axis of symmetry, with two Bs framing the doubled H, and to clarify its meaning. In 1687, a comma after "Bully" makes "Hector" something visibly separate (a swaggerer or, as in line 478, "a blustring wind"). In 1707, "humane Beast" becomes "human beast", better signalling that special sense of the adjective which allows the male beast to be "human/e" here ("in the form of a man") but "inhumane" ("devoid of all the qualities a man should have") in line 529.

126. ***Balaam's Ass:*** Balaam's ass was a beast that spoke (Numbers 22.28-30), and Egerton suggests that her opponent should be placed in the same category.

127. **Each act his part:** The masculine pronoun flies in the face of legend; the vengeful Furies were female deities.

128. **'Tis false in her, yet 'tis sum'd up in you:** In other words, you yourself epitomise everything that you have wrongly alleged is characteristic of women.

129. **You almost would perswade one that you thought ... :** The sentence which she embarks upon here sees Egerton affecting incredulity: "it is as if you really held the absurd belief that supply problems and a shortage of female souls had forced God into thriftily reallocating to one woman after another the souls originally bestowed upon the bad women of Biblical times, Jezebel and Eve".

130. **These later bodies:** The phrase was later emended to "These latter bodies" (1707).

131. **I'm no *Pythagorean*:** Pythagoras was associated with the theory of the transmigration of souls. As recalled by Malvolio in Act 4, Scene 2 of Shakespeare's *Twelfth Night*, "the opinion of Pythagoras" was that "the soul of our grandam might haply inhabit a bird".

132. ***Abraham* and *Jude*:** Abraham in the Old Testament was "a father of many nations" (Genesis 17.4-5); but anything of Abraham's would have to travel down an extremely long bloodline to reach Jude, who comes at the end of the New Testament; his epistle is the last book before Revelation.

133. **I must needs conceit their souls the same:** The meaning here is "I would have to fancy that they shared the souls of Jezebel and Eve"—whereas in fact we can feel "sure" that the women of today ("our Sex") are not contaminated by any such intermingling.

134. **I confess there's some that merit blame:** Compare line 264, "I must confess there are some bad ...".

135. **we're not made so perfect but may err ... :** In lines 413-23 Egerton extends to women John Milton's argument in his pamphlet *Areopagitica* (1644) that "that which purifies us is triall". If a woman's gravitation towards goodness (or abstention from evil) were preprogrammed, rather than a choice which she must consciously weigh, then she would only have—in Milton's words—"a blank virtue, not a pure".

136. **she has happiness:** This "happiness" of women is really their peculiar good fortune, to possess constitutions acutely responsive to promptings which are divine yet resistant to any which are not.

137. **pride and their lov'd luxury:** What in *Love given o're* were female attributes—"Folly, Falshood, Lux'ry, Lust, and Pride" (*LGO* 2)—are imputed by Egerton to men instead. "Luxury" at this time had a sense, lasciviousness or wantonness, which the word has since lost.

138. **their souls grow brave:** What Egerton goes on to say about the underhand means used by "th'ambitious" as they climb the ladder of court favour makes it clear that boldness or ruthlessness is meant here, rather than bravery as conventionally defined.

139. **And by grave Councels ... oft works their end:** The "grave Councels" are earnest speeches of the sort that ambitious court favourites will pour into a monarch's ear, hoping to

convince him that they have his best interests at heart. "Guilt poyson" presents problems, but "gilt" for "guilt" is a possible emendation; these speeches are gilded pills, effectively, with which "th'ambitious" find "a … fatal way to please" and manage to gloss over the death and destruction that they are administering.

140. **and then … his adherency:** Typically—having had the monarch accept, or "approve" (line 451), his advice that the popularity of the heir to the throne makes it essential to remove this threat—the favourite will proceed to press for all of the heir's followers to be, on the grounds of national security, likewise eliminated.

141. **the false usurper mounts the Throne:** A triplet brace in the original indicates that "Throne" is intended to rhyme with "room" and "Tomb". Lines 458-63 represent one of only two instances in Egerton's poem of *consecutive* triplets (the other occurring in lines 184-9), and are immediately followed by the unique spectacle of a single rhyme spread over five lines. Within the same hundred-line sequence which contains the present passage, moreover, are the only three cases in the poem of a single rhyme spread over *four* lines (lines 446-9, 509-12, 542-5).

142. **He nere sits firm:** Unlike the "nere" in line 371 (see note 119), this one was not emended until 1707—and then not to "ne'er" but to "ne're".

143. **Thus what I've said … than a woman far:** These two lines were later rewritten with the stress moved back from the second syllable of "impious" to the first: "And thus by what I've said, we plainly find/ That Men more impious are than Womankind" (1687).

144. **being uneasie:** Line 444, in which "not at ease" was synonymous with "restless", is helpful here. Rather than meaning "apprehensive", "uneasie" in the present context means "dissatisfied".

145. **Above them, in State:** The order of these two phrases was, for the sake of the metre, later reversed: "In State, above them …"(1687).

146. **In a degree that is above their own:** "Degree" in this context refers to rank, status, social class.

147. **Speaks thee nothing but a blustring wind:** The version of 1687 and 1707, "And speaks thee nothing but a blustring wind" (with "wind" taking a capital W in 1707), mends the faulty metre by filling out the first foot; but, if Egerton had

indeed originally begun with "Speaks", that restoration cancelled a sound instinct. Since the line without "And" is an emptier vessel, the sound seems a more resonant echo to the sense; and, across the open space which the missing syllable has left, the plosive Bs of the previous line can blow back—in "but a blustring wind"—with an even noisier huffing and puffing. (The noun "wind" has a long vowel and rhymes with "mind" not only for Egerton but for several later generations of writers; John Keats uses the rhyme in his "Ode to Psyche".)

148. **nor won't be imply'd:** The intended sense of "imply'd" (which in modern English would be better conveyed by "implicated") is "entangled".

149. **That my dull Arithmetick cannot tell/ Half the sins … :** metrically adjusted in 1687 to read: "My dull Arithmetick can never tell/ Half of the sins …".

150. **one sordid Rustick:** The "sordid Rustick" is a humble peasant; and, given that she cannot gauge even his levels of pride and lustfulness, how much higher—Egerton asks—are those levels likely to be among men with more so-called politeness, refinement, and sophistication?

151. **But theirs is running over and prest down:** This rather repetitive rumination on the boundlessness of male pride was replaced in the 1687 edition by the stronger line "But 'tis too great a Task for me alone".

152. **this doth insnare:** The comma after "insnare", unwanted because it comes between a verb and its direct object, was dropped from the 1687 edition.

153. **he doth still pursue … surely be abhorr'd:** Lustful men are incapable of reciprocating the love of a wife, Egerton argues, because they are impelled continually to look beyond it and pursue all those who arouse their desires. Theoretically, if polygamy were permitted, it would provide some sort of sanction or cover for their lust; but in practice the number of wives would make no difference since sexual pleasure for such men lies always outside marriage.

154. **And some common *Lais* be ador'd:** Lais is taken to typify the courtesan; it was in Corinth that she famously plied her trade. (See Illustration number 2.) The later version of this line, "And still some common *Lais* be adored" (1687), adds a syllable to correct the metre.

155. **So, for by ends,/ They take a Wife:** If men who are lustful marry at all, Egerton suggests, it is for purely opportunistic reasons. (Bunyan's Mr By-ends, in *The Pilgrim's Progress*, will

do whatever is expedient.) What they want is to establish a clear line of succession. All they achieve is complete confusion over the inheritance that they are handing down, with the legitimate pitted against the illegitimate issue.

156. **he perhaps at last:** The pronoun has a double reference; behind the generic "he"—indicating the type of man, wherever he might be found, who is lustful—lurks the individual case of Egerton's "Antagonist", the author of *LGO*, whose lust she has supposed to surpass that of other men (line 83).

157. **I could say more:** The same rhetorical refusal to specify (in effect an attempt, by drawing veils, to convince the reader that there is something very impressive concealed behind them) was seen in line 135.

158. **that do not die:** This was grammatically corrected, in 1707, to "that does not die".

159. **Bewley's Pox:** According to *LGO* (4), when "Bewley" died "all her Body was one putrid Sore,/ Studded with Pox, and Ulcers quite all o're".

160. **Men do catch it by meer phantasie:** Egerton means that, if one is to believe all that men say, they never actually do anything to contract syphilis; it simply communicates itself to them as if through the air.

161. **and some company ... hast'neth their death:** The first nine words of this are elliptical (or corrupt); but the meaning of the passage is clarified by the 1687 revisions:

> while they swear it with an oath
> 'Twas only in Company, infected breath
> Gave them that *Plague*, which hastens on their death ...

In other words, those who have contracted syphilis protest that it was only an airborne contagion transmitted to them by others with whom they had happened to associate.

162. **a sum of Money must be gave ... And then 'tis doubled:** The physician is party to the deception, and there is therefore a need for payment to keep him quiet, on top of the payment due to him for the treatment of the condition itself. (Despite its proximity to "cheat" and "deceit", which may tempt us to understand it as fraud, the "corruption" in fact is physical and syphilitic.)

163. **And then the only Objects ... make them conceal:** The last of these lines was polished by slight subsequent revision: "What Money doth oblige 'em to conceal" (1687). After the silence of all those in the know has been bought, the dying man has no money left to leave.

164. **These are partakers … :** This passage, over the space of almost sixteen lines, ponders the relative guilt of those who commit a crime and the accomplices who hypocritically sweep it under the carpet. There is little to choose between them, Egerton proposes, except that the latter—who carefully cover up the wrong they have done—cannot incite other "mad Souls" to do likewise. The full stop between "strives to win" and "Mad Souls" (lines 566-7) is an error, since the sense is continuous, and is dropped from the 1687 edition.

165. **Than one of these is better than the t'other:** The 1687 and 1707 texts confirm that the first "Than" should really be a "Then"; but at this time the boundary between "Than" and "Then" was quite indistinctly drawn (see also note 107).

166. **Hypocrisie preheminence should have:** It was once common to spell "pre-eminence" (if unhyphenated) with an "h". The extra letter simply did the work of a diæresis, ensuring that the second "e" was sounded separately from the first.

167. **Seem more smooth … more pardonable:** The second edition (1687) makes the metre smoother and less rugged by adding two extra syllables to the first of these lines and reversing the word order at the beginning of the next: "Seem much more smooth, and a vile common sin/ More pardonable look". Since "pardonable" behaves like "inseparable" in line 653 (see note 192), its penultimate syllable is stressed.

168. **But should there be … :** Egerton argues in lines 567-78 that men whose virtuous behaviour is based only upon their imitation of what appears virtue in others can neither be given any credit for such behaviour nor be expected to remain true to it under pressure.

169. **Nothing e're acted but Hypocrisie:** Just as "nere" or "ne're" corresponds to modern English "never" (see notes 119 and 142), so "ere" or "e're" corresponds to modern English "ever" (see also note 81).

170. **without pattern, never had imbrac't:** Chastity is understood here, as the thing which—but for the instruction derived from what pass for positive instances of the same—would never have been embraced.

171. **Such kind of sins … will break:** The meaning of this couplet is clearer, and the movement less awkward, in the 1687 edition: "Such kind of force at best, such virtue's weak,/ That streight with such a slender stress will break".

172. **the *Grecian*:** The reference is to the Greek philosopher Diogenes, supposed to have gone on his travels with a lantern and used it to search (in vain) for an honest man.

173. **it with Justice went/ Up thither:** "It" is still honesty—which, together with Justice, has fled from this world to the next. The myth of Astraea, the goddess of justice, has her departing from the earth in despair and ascending to the stars.

174. **here is found no content ... past by:** "Content" is to be understood in the largest possible sense, including (like Greek *eudaimonia*) ethical joy, psychic harmony, and a profound sense of inner wellbeing. Nobody finds this here, Egerton suggests; in fact, we positively turn away from it and so are shockingly wide of the mark.

175. **brag of their horrid Facts:** The "Facts" are the crimes committed by Egerton's male reprobates. These men are completely brazen about their wrongdoing except where they fear being disinherited on account of it.

176. **some other way they'l drive/ Their golden wheels:** Since these "Mad Souls" are destined to fill up hell (line 567), Egerton may be alluding to the golden chariot in which Hades—King of the Underworld—was traditionally represented as riding.

177. **his Lusts:** "His Lusts" are the courtesans and mistresses with whom he would take his pleasures, whereas "his pretended Joy" (line 601) is the wife whom he pretends to love—but whom he robs (lines 601-603) of bequests that were meant for her alone.

178. **And their great kindness turn'd an abuse:** metrically adjusted in 1687 to read "And their great kindness turn'd to an abuse".

179. *Sisiphus* **his fate:** Sisyphus' fate, which for the sake of the metre Egerton expresses not with the *–s* but with the *his* genitive (either was possible at this time), was endlessly to roll a stone up a hill and then see it roll back down again. What the comparison conveys is that, as soon as Egerton had finished rehearsing all she knew about the falsehood of men, there would be just as many fresh instances to enumerate; it is impossible for the catalogue of shame ever to catch up with all that men do.

180. **Infidelity:** "Infidelity" serves in this context as a general term for "breach of promise"; sexual unfaithfulness is not the dominant seventeenth-century sense.

181. *Egypt's* **false King** *Ptolomy*: Ptolemy's act of betrayal came to be described rather differently in the 1687 and 1707 editions of *FA*, where line 617 was revised as follows: "Approv'd his Death, and Murderer let go free". In the interests of historical accuracy, Egerton decided to portray Ptolemy not as a killer but as the accomplice in a killing.

182. **He was inconstant ... words not mind:** One possibility entertained by Egerton, therefore, is that Ptolemy—having made Pompey this promise, and meant it at first—had second thoughts and decided that he would break it. Another is that he had never (not even at the outset) intended to keep it, in which case what he had said was a lie because he went back on it with no intervening change of mind to palliate the perfidy. ("So alter'd words not mind" is elliptical for "and so altered his words but not his mind".)

183. **With a full resolution, for to break:** Strictly speaking, since the breaking of the word and oath is what has been resolved upon, the line needs to be left unpunctuated. The comma after "resolution" was accordingly dropped in the process of revision (1707).

184. **One's word and oath ... failing in the soul:** Two of these three lines, like many others in *FA*, are a syllable short of what is required for metrical regularity. The necessary adjustment was made in 1687:

    One's word and oath, most surely it must be
    A greater crime than an inconstancy,
    Which is as great a failing in the soul ...

185. **must/ Be sure ... for to remove:** Egerton feels obliged, she says, to adhere to her original intention of not venturing too far into the "lab'rinth" (lines 479f); otherwise she will find herself needing to root out in herself the very fault (that of being "a Talkative") which she rebukes in others.

186. *Brutus* **... ought to have been** *Caesar's* **friend:** According to Mark Antony in Act 3 Scene 2 of Shakespeare's *Julius Caesar*, the fact that Brutus had been "Caesar's angel" made the wound which Brutus's dagger inflicted "the most unkindest cut of all".

187. **nay and disloyal too:** As in line 639—and, further afield, in line 369—Egerton favours a form of rhetorical correction (metanoia) in which a term is used only to be immediately trumped by another that is more precise or more to the point.

188. **More unconstant, nay and more perfidious:** This claim is later scaled up, even as the length and rhythm of the line are regularised: "Far more unconstant, nay perfidious" (1687).

189. **But these are Crimes ... 'tis as false as they:** That is, although men claim that failings such as inconstancy are defining characteristics of women this is an allegation as false as men are. The phrase "hath peculiar given/ Unto our Sex" (i.e., "has foisted particularly, or purely, upon women") becomes, in the 1687 edition, "hath in peculiar given / Unto our Sex".

190. **'Tis she must bear sins of all the land:** metrically adjusted in 1687 to read "'Tis she must bear the sins of all the land".
191. **he himself:** i.e., the priest.
192. **inseparable/ To men o'th' Gown:** "Inseparable" formerly took either "from" or "to". (The *Oxford English Dictionary* cites Richard Steele, writing in 1712: "Ingratitude is a Vice inseparable to a lustful Man.") Egerton's rhyme with "Table" reflects the tendency for writers of her and Steele's generation to stress the penultimate syllable of any adjective formed with the suffix *–able*. In *Cadenus and Vanessa*, lines 550-51, Jonathan Swift (1667–1745) writes: "But time, and books, and state affairs/ Had spoil'd his fashionable airs".
193. **I must not look in my Teachers lives:** The editions of both 1687 and 1707 again add the requisite tenth syllable: "I must not look into my Teachers lives". Little is known of the religious instruction received by Egerton personally; but children up and down the land were expected to learn the Anglican catechism (as revised and reaffirmed in 1662) at the hands of a curate.
194. **he doth not act all flame ... not a grant/ Of Objects:** Men may not always exhibit lust, Egerton says, "fierce" though its flames certainly are (line 526); but this is only because there might not always be suitable opportunities, or victims, for them to seize and exploit.
195. **He doth to any thing it doth desire:** Rather than altering "to" to "do", as might have been expected, the 1687 and 1707 editions replace "doth" with "yields".
196. **then they'd disobey:** That is, only if the "hellish fire" in their loins commanded them to be "good" (or, in this context, continent) would they disregard it.
197. **I am not sorry you do Females hate:** For the final nineteen lines of the poem Egerton reverts to directly addressing her "Antagonist", the author of *LGO*.
198. **at enmity with all that's good:** Egerton has already stated (line 373) that modesty is her opponent's "foe".
199. **'Tis an impossible:** The editions of 1687 and 1707 correct the misprint and rescue the comparison ("'Tis *as* impossible ...", emphasis mine).
200. **that's repugnancy:** i.e., that would be a logical contradiction.
201. **makes most Females brave:** "Brave" is used here, not to mean "courageous" or "intrepid", but in the looser sense of "excellent". The rhyme of "have" and "brave" also occurs in lines 442-3.

202. **lie in vast eternity:** This line exiles Egerton's "Antagonist" not just from pleasure but, perpetually, from bliss. The power of the phrase "vast eternity", a familiar one in seventeenth-century poetry, always came—according to Nigel Smith, glossing it in his edition of *The Poems of Andrew Marvell*, 82—from "its exclusion of any idea of romantic or theological afterlife".

203. **Woman, your imagin'd Fiend:** Egerton ties the conclusion of *FA* back to its beginning by returning to the trumped-up charge which her poem initially sought to counter: that "Some Curst or Banisht Fiend usurp't the way/ When *Eve* was form'd" (lines 2-3).

WORKS CITED AND CONSULTED

The following list contains works useful for a broad understanding of *The Female Advocate* and its context. In addition, where these—or other—works have helped on specific points and issues, those details are recorded in the appropriate note.

Barash, Carol. *English Women's Poetry, 1649–1714: Politics, Community, and Linguistic Authority.* 2nd ed. Oxford: Clarendon Press, 1996.

Capern, Amanda. *The Historical Study of Women: England 1500–1700.* Basingstoke: Palgrave Macmillan, 2007.

Chaucer, Geoffrey. *The Works of Geoffrey Chaucer.* Ed. F. N. Robinson, 2nd ed. London: Oxford UP, 1966.

[Egerton, Sarah.] *The Female Advocate: or, an Answer to A Late Satyr against The Pride, Lust and Inconstancy, &c. of Woman. Written by a Lady in Vindication of her Sex.* London, 1686.

Ezell, Margaret J. M. "'By a Lady': The Mask of the Feminine in Restoration, Early Eighteenth-Century Print Culture", in *The Faces of Anonymity: Anonymous and Pseudonymous Publication from the Sixteenth to the Twentieth Century.* Ed. Robert J. Griffin. New York and Basingstoke: Palgrave Macmillan, 2003. 63-79.

Fairer, David and Christine Gerrard (eds). *Eighteenth-Century Poetry: An Annotated Anthology.* Oxford: Blackwell, 1999.

[Gould, Robert.] *Love given o're: or a Satyr against the Pride, Lust, and Inconstancy, &c. of Woman.* London, 1682/3.

Greene, Richard. "Egerton, Sarah (1670–1723)", in *The Oxford Dictionary of National Biography.* 60 vols. Ed. H. C. G. Matthew and Brian Harrison. Oxford: Oxford UP, 2004. 17: 1005.

Hardy, Barbara. "The Talkative Woman in Shakespeare, Dickens and George Eliot", in *Problems for Feminist Criticism*, ed. Sally Minogue (London: Routledge, 1990), 15-45.

Hobby, Elaine. *Virtue of Necessity: English Women's Writing 1649–88*. London: Virago, 1988.

Johnson, Samuel. *Lives of the English Poets*. 2 vols. Ed. Arthur Waugh. London: Oxford UP, 1906.

Kelly, Joan. "Early Feminist Theory and the 'Querelle des Femmes', 1400–1789", *Signs* 8.1 (1982), 4-28.

Kowalewski-Wallace, Elizabeth. *Their Fathers' Daughters: Hannah More, Maria Edgeworth, and Patriarchal Complicity*. New York and Oxford: Oxford UP, 1991.

Lonsdale, Roger (ed.). *Eighteenth-Century Women Poets: An Oxford Anthology*. Oxford and New York: Oxford UP, 1990.

Medoff, Joslyn. "New Light on Sarah Fyge (Field, Egerton)", *Tulsa Studies in Women's Literature* 1.2 (1982), 155-75.

Nolan, Michael. "The Mysterious Affair at Mâcon: The Bishops and the Souls of Women", *New Blackfriars* 74 (November 1993), 501-507.

Norris, Margot. "Stifled Back Answers: The Gender Politics of Art in Joyce's *The Dead*", *Modern Fiction Studies* 35.3 (1989), 479-506.

Nussbaum, Felicity A. *The Brink of All We Hate: English Satires on Women 1660–1750*. Lexington: UP of Kentucky, 1984.

Ostovich, Helen and Elizabeth Sauer, assisted by Melissa Smith (eds). *Reading Early Modern Women: An Anthology of Texts in Manuscript and Print, 1550–1700*. New York and London: Routledge, 2004.

Price, Bronwen. "Women's Poetry 1550–1700: 'Not Unfit to be Read'", in *A Companion to Early Modern Women's Writing*. Ed. Anita Pacheco. Oxford: Blackwell, 2002. 282-302.

Runge, Laura L. (ed.). *Texts from the Querelle 1641–1701 (1)*, vol. 3 of *Essential Works for the Study of Early Modern Women*: Part

2, in Series III of *The Early Modern Englishwoman: A Facsimile Library of Essential Works*. Aldershot: Ashgate, 2007.

Smith, Hilda L. *Reason's Disciples: Seventeenth-Century English Feminists*. Urbana, Chicago, and London: University of Illinois Press, 1982.

Smith, Nigel (ed.). *The Poems of Andrew Marvell*. Harlow: Pearson, 2007.

Steele, Richard. "The Spectator, Tuesday, 13 March 1711", in *Selections from "The Tatler" and "The Spectator"*. Ed. Angus Ross. Harmondsworth: Penguin Books, 1982. 463-7.

Teague, Frances and Rebecca De Haas. "Defences of Women", in *A Companion to Early Modern Women's Writing*. Ed. Anita Pacheco. Oxford: Blackwell, 2002. 248-63.

Todd, Janet. *The Sign of Angellica: Women, Writing, and Fiction 1660-1800*. London: Virago Press, 1989.

Tomalin, Claire. *The Life and Death of Mary Wollstonecraft*. Harmondsworth: Penguin Books, 1977.

Wiesner, Merry E. *Women and Gender in Early Modern Europe*. Cambridge: Cambridge University Press, 1993.

Wilson, John Harold (ed.). *Court Satires of the Restoration*. Columbus: Ohio State University Press, 1976.

Yeats, W. B. *The Major Works: Including Poems, Plays, and Critical Prose*. Ed. Edward Larrissy. Oxford: Oxford UP, 2001.

A key resource from 2010, by which the present volume was unable to benefit because it went to press too soon, will be a facsimile edition of the printed writings of Sarah Fyge Egerton, selected and introduced by Robert C. Evans and joining Laura L. Runge's *Texts from the Querelle* in the Ashgate *Early Modern Englishwoman* series.

Juvenilia
PRESS
Catalogue

GENERAL EDITOR: Christine Alexander

Available volumes can be purchased via the Juvenilia Press website:
www.arts.unsw.edu.au/juvenilia/

Volumes in the series:

- *Jack & Alice*, by Jane Austen at age c.13. Edited by Juliet Mc-Master and others. 1992, 1994.

- *The Twelve Adventurers: A Romance*, by Charlotte Brontë at 13. Edited by Juliet McMaster and others. 1993, 1994.

- *Amelia Webster and The Three Sisters*, by Jane Austen at c.13 and 16. Edited by Juliet McMaster and others. 1993, 1995.

- *Indamora to Lindamira*, by Lady Mary Pierrepont (later Wortley Montagu) at c.14. Edited by Isobel Grundy, with Susan Hillabold. 1994. First publication.

- *Norna, or The Witch's Curse*, by Louisa May Alcott at c.15. Edited by Juliet McMaster and others. 1994.

- *Pockets Full of Stars*, by Alison White from age 13. Edited by Arlette Zinck. 1994.

- *Branwell's Blackwoods Magazine*, by Branwell Brontë at 11. Edited by Christine Alexander, with Vanessa Benson. 1995. First publication.

- *The History of England*, by Jane Austen at 15. Edited by Jan Fergus and others. 1995, 2003.

- *Love and Freindship*, by Jane Austen at 14. Edited by Juliet McMaster and others. 1995, 2006, 2008.

- *Edward Neville*, by George Eliot at 14. Edited by Juliet McMaster and others. 1995. Revised edition, 2009.

Catalogue

- *Catharine, or The Bower*, by Jane Austen at 16. Edited by Juliet McMaster and others. 1996, 2005.
- *Henry and Eliza*, by Jane Austen at c.13. Edited by Karen L. Hartnick and others. 1996.
- *A Quiet Game*, by Margaret Atwood at c.17. Edited by Kathy Chung and Sherrill Grace. 1997 (First publication), 2006.
- *The Young Visiters*, by Daisy Ashford at 9. Edited by Juliet McMaster and others. 1997. (not available for sale)
- *My Angria and the Angrians*, by Charlotte Brontë at 18. Edited by Juliet McMaster, Leslie Robertson and others. 1997.
- *Embryo Words*, by Margaret Laurence from age 14. Edited by Nora Foster Stovel and others. 1997.
- *A Collection of Letters*, by Jane Austen at c.16. Edited by Juliet McMaster and others. 1998, 2006.
- *Lesley Castle*, by Jane Austen at c.15. Edited by Jan Fergus and others. 1998, 2006.
- *Satan in a Barrel, and other early stories*, by Malcolm Lowry at 16. Edited by Sherrill Grace. 1999.
- *Evelyn*, by Jane Austen at 16. Edited by Peter Sabor and others. 1999.
- *Albion and Marina*, by Charlotte Brontë at 14. Edited by Juliet McMaster and others. 1999.
- *Colors of Speech*, by Margaret Laurence at 19-20. Edited by Nora Foster Stovel and others. 2000. First publication.
- *The Adventurer*, by Lady Mary Pierrepont (later Wortley Montagu) at 14. Edited by Isobel Grundy and others. 2000. First publication.

Juvenilia PRESS

Catalogue

- *Early Voices*, by Greg Hollingshead, Carol Shields, Aritha van Herk, and Ruby Wiebe. Edited by T.L. Walters and James King. 2001. First publication.

- *Jack & Alice*, by Jane Austen at c.13. Edited by Joseph Wiesenfarth, with Laura Maestrelli and Kristin Smith. 2001.

- *Peter Paul Rubens and Other Friendly Folk*, by Opal Whiteley, at 6-7. Edited by Laura Cappello, Juliet McMaster, Lesley Peterson, and Chris Wagner. 2001.

- *Tales of the Islanders, Volume 1*, by Charlotte Brontë at 13. Edited by Christine Alexander and others. 2001, 2006.

- *Sunbeams from a Golden Machine*, by Marian Engel at 16. Edited by Afra Kavanagh and Tammy MacNeil. 2002.

- *Frederic & Elfrida*, by Jane Austen at 11 or 12. Edited by Peter Sabor, Sylvia Hunt and Victoria Kortes-Papp. 2002.

- *Tales of the Islanders, Volume 2*, by Charlotte Brontë at 13. Edited by Christine Alexander and others. 2002, 2006.

- *Incidents from Phippy's Schooldays*, by Philip Larkin at c.15. Edited by Brenda Allen and James Acheson. 2002. First publication.

- *Tales of the Islanders, Volume 3*, by Charlotte Brontë at 14. Edited by Christine Alexander and others. 2003.

- *Artless Tales*, by Anna Maria Porter at 13. Edited by Leslie Robertson, Lesley Peterson, and Juliet McMaster. 2003. First publication since 1793.

- *The Three Sisters*, by Jane Austen at c.16. Edited by Joseph Wiesenfarth, Laura Maestrelli and Kristin Smith. 2004.

- *The Diary of Iris Vaughan*, written from age 7. Edited by Peter Alexander and Peter Midgley. 2004.

Catalogue

- *Tales of the Islanders, Volume 4*, by Charlotte Brontë at 14. Edited by Christine Alexander and others. 2005.
- *Lady Susan*, by Jane Austen at c.18. Edited by Christine Alexander and David Owen. 2005.
- *Three Mini-Dramas*, by Jane Austen at c.12, 13 and 17. Edited by Juliet McMaster, Lesley Peterson and others. 2006.
- *Dick Doyle's Journal*, by Richard Doyle at 15. Edited by Juliet McMaster and others. 2006.
- *Jane Austen's Men*, by Jane Austen at c.12 to 14. Edited by Sylvia Hunt and others. 2007.
- *Dick Doyle's Journal, Volume 2*, by Richard Doyle at 15. Edited by Juliet McMaster and others. 2008.
- *The Rectory Magazine*, by Lewis Carroll at c.15. Edited by Valerie Sanders and Elizabeth O'Reilly. 2008.
- *The Gipsy Dancer & Early Poems*, by Dorothy Hewett at age 7–12. Edited by Christine Alexander and others. 2009.
- *Dick Doyle's Journal, Volume 3*, by Richard Doyle at 15-16. Edited by Juliet McMaster, Amy Stafford, and others. 2009.
- *The History of England & Cassandra's Portraits*, by Jane Austen at 15. Edited by Annette Upfal and Christine Alexander. 2009.
- *The Female Advocate*, by Sarah Fyge Egerton at 14-16. Edited by Peter Merchant, with Steven Orman. 2010.